WHEN THE BODY DISPLACES THE MIND

WHEN THE BODY DISPLACES THE MIND

STRESS, TRAUMA AND SOMATIC DISEASE

Jean Benjamin Stora

Foreword by Mark Solms

Translated by Sophie Leighton

KARNAC

First published in 2007 by
Karnac Books Ltd.
118 Finchley Road, London NW3 5HT

Copyright © 2007 by Jean Benjamin Stora
English language copyright © Sophie Leighton 2007

The rights of Jean Benjamin Stora to be identified as the author of this work have been asserted in accordance with §§ 77 and 78 of the Copyright Design and Patents Act 1988.

British Library Cataloguing in Publication Data

A C.I.P. for this book is available from the British Library
ISBN-13: 978-1-85575-418-8

Typeset by Vikatan Publishing Solutions, Chennai, India

Printed in Great Britain

www.karnacbooks.com

CONTENTS

v

vi   CONTENTS

For Judith and Michael

FOREWORD

The boundaries between disciplines have recently been seriously challenged in the neurosciences. This has resulted, among other things, in a realisation that the brain cannot be understood in isolation from other bodily organs. This realisation, in turn, has produced important advances in neuro-endocrinology and neuro-immunology, to mention only the obvious instances. But certainly one of the most significant advances brought about by this development has been in the scientific understanding of *emotion*. Few neuroscientists today would deny that the brain mechanisms of emotion (and drive) are centrally embedded in brain: body relationships.

According to the currently dominant view, emotions are conceptualised as evaluative neural registrations of the visceral body's current state. This conceptualisation reflects the truism (all too easily forgotten) that the essential function of the brain is to represent the state of the body – of both its sensory end-organs and its endogenous visceral detectors – and then, drawing on past experience, to 'compute' appropriate efferent responses to this state. These efferent responses, no less than the inputs that trigger them, are of two types: both external and internal. In the latter (internal) responses we find the common origin of many (if not most) of the complex phenomena that are grouped together clinically under the heading of 'psychosomatic medicine'.

It is very much to the credit of contemporary neuroscience that it has found a place for psychoanalysis in this interdisciplinary vortex, and it is likewise fortunate indeed that psychoanalysis (under the banner of 'neuro-psychoanalysis') has been able to rise to the occasion, and make some significant contributions to the avalanche of neuroscientific discoveries that are now reported almost daily. These contributions have been limited almost exclusively to revealing the role of unconscious emotional processes in so-called neurobehavioural (or neuropsychological) syndromes. We therefore have reason to be grateful to Professor Stora for this pioneering volume, in which he makes a first neuro-psychoanalytic foray into the fascinating and important field of psychosomatic medicine. In this spirit, I unequivocally recommend his work to prospective readers, and encourage his colleagues to take up the many scientific challenges he poses for them here.

Mark Solms
Cape Town and London, November 2006

ACKNOWLEDGEMENTS

I should like to express my thanks to the following: Dr Alain Braconnier, who has supported my research endeavours throughout the last few years; Professors Jean-François Allilaire, Pierre Bourgeois, Gérard Turpin, Eric Bruckert and André Grimaldi, who have kindly allowed me to conduct psychosomatic investigations in various departments at La Pitié-Salpétrière teaching hospital – all of whom I would like to thank for their openness to ideas and scientific collaboration. My thanks also go to Drs Philippe Giral and Sylvain Mimoun and to Professors David Ruelle, Gilles Mauffrey,[1] Tobie Nathan and Alain Blanchet, who in various ways have furthered my research in the field of psychosomatics.

I should also like to thank my students on the diploma in clinical psychology and psychopathology at the University of Paris VIII, the patients who have given me permission to use illustrative material in this book, whose anonymity I have preserved, and the senior administrative staff and nurses in the various departments in which I have worked – without all these people and friends, this book would have been impossible for me to write.

Finally I would like to thank my wife, Professor Judith Stora-Sandor, of the University of Paris VIII, who has borne with my extensive periods of work throughout the last five years, provided encouragement at difficult times, and with whom I have discussed all the clinical and theoretical aspects of my research, as well as my son Michael, a psychologist and psychoanalyst, who has read through many parts of this book and asked me pertinent questions on each occasion.

Jean Benjamin Stora
Paris, February 2007

Introduction

"The body itself, simply from the laws of its own nature, can do many things which its mind wonders at ... it is in the mind's power alone both to speak and to be silent and to do many other things which they therefore believe depend on the mind's decision ... if, on the other hand, the body is inactive, the mind is at the same time incapable of thinking".

[Spinoza, *The Ethics*. [II/142, p. 72]

Some questions concerning illness and death

I was confronted with the problem of severe illness and death at a very early age; ever since then, I have been concerned with questions relating to the diseased body and the mind and their connections and to what I referred to as the soul. This early experience at the age of eleven years left a deep impression on me and indirectly determined my career path as a practitioner of psychoanalysis and psychosomatics; I became a clinical psychologist rather than a medical doctor. Today I work as a psychologist in a white coat alongside my medical colleagues in order to investigate the psychic dimension in somatic patients and to put forward a wide range of psychotherapeutic treatments on a joint and complementary basis to medical treatments.

"A childhood memory"

I witnessed my grandfather's terrible suffering from cancer when I was only a small child. A specific event seemed to lie at the origin of this illness–at least, that was my understanding of its cause: one of my cousins had had a horrible accident. He had been run over by an army lorry while he was crossing the road in the district where we were living. The violent emotion engendered by this traumatic event left a permanent mark on me; mourning is an impressive spectacle in Mediterranean countries. I remember my grandfather beating his chest and the traditional female mourners crying. Was this the event that had precipitated this illness? Was it possible for an emotion to cause an illness and subsequent death? I actually observed the gradual deterioration in my grandfather's health he resisted the disease by reading his book of the psalms of David, as tradition prescribed for a religious man. At a much later stage, I understood the deep impact that religious tradition has on people's psychic lives and I carefully read all the commentaries relating to disease and cure. The question posed by Jewish Biblical commentators is as follows: "When a man is ill, should he turn directly to God or should he consult a doctor?" The answers to this are long and complex in the Judaeo-Christian tradition to which I am referring, as one of the two foundation stones of Western European cultural values. I know that the Christian theological dimension is often quoted as a source and, as I am slightly more familiar with the Jewish tradition, this is the one to which I shall refer. My grandfather would read night and day; as I watched him sadly, I somehow felt that this might be helping him. I have never since doubted that the spiritual dimension plays an important role in restoring individual psychosomatic equilibrium for those who have received a spiritual education. Moreover, there are two different answers to the question posed above: either that those who put their trust in God have no need of doctors (Maimonides, Moses ben Maimon–Rambam, 1135–1204, Vayikra commentaries 26, 11) or that medical treatment is a basic human need of the same order as eating or breathing and that it would be mad to advise a starving man to wait for a miracle instead of feeding himself (Rambam, commentary on Mishna, Pessa'him, 4). Other commentaries state that the recourse to God is reserved for the Righteous–now who in our day is a Righteous one? I think that my grandfather, highly conscious of the limitations of the medicine of his time and as a traditional believer, was making recourse to existing practices. I can still see him now leaning over his prayer-book.

As his health continued to decline, one day to my great surprise I saw some traditional healers arriving at the house; they were said to be the inheritors of ancient and mysterious healing practices. I have to say that I felt some embarrassment at this visitation, but then if it might help my grandfather, why not? Later, reading the works of the great mediaeval doctor Maimonides, I understood the underlying reasons for my attitude. I knew intuitively that magical practices (wearing amulets, secret prayers, foreign customs and so on) were contrary to the spirit of Judaism, but I also somehow knew that they were difficult to root out because they corresponded to a cultural and psychic need.[2] The final endeavours to cure him failed and my grandfather died. I accompanied him to his last resting place, carrying his coffin over a long distance in ritual fashion, along with my family, and it was at his tomb that I understood that the body disappeared for ever to return to the dust from which it came. If death were a certainty, since that was the law, what became of our soul and our mind?

I think that this was when I first began to wonder about the possible causal connections, while questioning Leibniz's form of causalist determinism–the metaphysical doctrine that every event has an antecedent, "a cause" without which it could not exist. This approach is based on a fatalistic world view with which I was rather too familiar and not especially comfortable; this was akin to the well-known "mektub" of Muslims. This elimination of freedom by a metaphysical causalism prompted me at an early age to explore the study of probability and uncertainty in the observation of human behaviour.

I think that it was back then that I tacitly inferred that although the soul might border on divinity, our non-material mind, always present in external life, vanished with our body; this too returned to dust. The mind was part of the material body. How then did the mind and the body communicate? Could the mind cause diseases?

Objectives and methodological approach

My aim in this book is to answer these questions and to propose a comprehensive approach for doctors and psychotherapists, those treating somatic patients whether in hospitals or private practice. I am also setting out to raise awareness among readers with an interest in new developments and fresh approaches to diseases and patients.

In this work, I am seeking to demonstrate the interrelations between mind and body with reference to various scientific disciplines.

At the beginning of the 21st century, an integration of the least material element of human beings, namely the psyche or, to be more precise, the psychic apparatus, into medical knowledge and clinical expertise is long overdue. It is important that this should no longer be considered either as a secondary factor in somatisations by doctors or as the main factor in somatisations by psychoanalysts who are psychosomaticians. The formulation of the problematics has to be reconsidered. The clinical profile of all diseases needs to incorporate this psychic component in its dynamic interrelations with functions and organs rather than allowing it to feature apparently unconnectedly alongside somatic elements in clinical reports in medical journals and books. The psychic apparatus forms part of the functional processes of living organisms; it is, in fact, the only characteristic that distinguishes human beings from all the other living species on the planet and, as we know, it takes nearly two decades from birth for this non-material element to become established. The unbalanced evolution of the sciences has led to "the medicine of the body" developing over the last two and a half millennia, with psychoanalysis emerging only at the end of the 19th century, providing for the first time in history with Sigmund Freud scientific concepts that made it possible to describe psychic processes and offer new forms of treatment for mental and neural disorders. However, the approaches are still highly disparate; doctors and epidemiologists consider the psychoanalytic approach to be too subjective and clinical to become a science with reliable and universally accepted concepts.

I am of course generalising but these are arguments that I have often encountered in my professional practice.

In the 1930s and 1940s, the psychosomatic medical approach put forward by Franz Alexander (1950) and Flanders-Dunbar (1935) among others provided a preliminary scientific model to account for somatisations, either emphasising a psychogenesis of illnesses or putting forward personality profiles based on susceptibility to specific illnesses—the seven famous so-called psychosomatic diseases studied by doctors and psychoanalysts at the Chicago Institute.[3]

This model persists to this day in debates concerning the problem of body-mind relations; however, it has now been partly superseded and replaced by other approaches. Privileging the psyche as a causal factor in somatic illnesses is in some ways as one-sided as privileging an organ, function or somatic system as an explanatory factor in diseases: the reality is more complex and more comprehensive and therefore what is required is an approach that integrates every aspect of the living organism.

This rigorous approach was developed in France by Pierre Marty and his colleagues, who founded what became known as the Paris School of Psychosomatics in the 1960s. They have since pursued their investigations, with some having left the field or abandoned this path of enquiry and others having continued the work along various lines. Marty constructed an explanatory model for the interrelation between psychic and somatic processes. He thereby proposed a theoretical and clinical formulation that was lacking in psychosomatics. Without losing sight of the clinical investigation, he created a "classification" incorporating the main concepts that provide a means of assessing psychic functioning as well as an epidemiological approach (Stora, 1994, 1995).[4] He thereby opened the first line of communication between medicine and psychoanalysis.

Both doctors and psychoanalysts who are psychosomaticians may be confronted with many disorders that determine their respective fields of intervention and reinforce the epistemological splitting instead of the approach that I am recommending.

As we can observe, the traditional medical approach today still distinguishes between so-called real illnesses, that is to say lesional ones, and so-called false ones, namely functional disorders. This latter observation ties in with the opposition between a medical treatment that focuses on the diseased organ and a medicine that focuses on the diseased person. Surveys conducted among people who have consulted general practitioners reveal that 50–70% of patients do not have lesional illnesses (Jeammet, Reynaud & Consoli, 1996). The doctor's initial response when faced with a non-lesional disorder may be: "This is nothing because it is not lesional". However, in that case what is the patient suffering from? What is the role played by the suffering that accompanies the pain? Alternatively, what is the role played by pain without suffering? Or is it that in order to be acknowledged as valid by a doctor, the patient has to present a series of somatic disorders until one of them is acknowledged as relevant by the doctor? As for functional disorders, these are the privileged site of expression for some patients who use their body as a means of communicating with the doctor; these have given rise to "psycho-somatic theories" that draw on metaphor and imaginary representations in order to ascribe a meaning to somatic symptoms. However, an explanation in terms of the imaginary and the symbolic does not account for the phenomena of somatisations that conform to laws that take some account of this mode of expression but also include other elements from several somatic and psychic systems.

It would be possible to group together, completely intertwined, this spectrum of disorders that relate to almost every aspect of medicine and psychoanalysis under the heading "psychosomatic"; *but this designation does not cover all the phenomena that I would like to address in this book* because it almost always carries a connotation of psychic pseudo-causality–this is a term that I shall often be using for want of a better one.

I favour a multi-causal approach to somatic patients; human beings are fundamentally integrated in three inextricable dimensions: *a somatic, a psychic and a socio-cultural dimension.*

The causes of an illness may lie in any one of the three dimensions and their interrelations must prompt practitioners–be they doctors, psychologists or institutional care workers–to assess their consequences for the ensuing imbalances in the human being. Every therapeutic endeavour ideally should incorporate these three dimensions.

The human being, as Marty expressed it, is "psychosomatic by definition".

The hypothesis that I am putting forward in this book is as follows: in relation to the psychic functioning of somatic patients, all the reflections of Freud and Marty lead to privileging "the economic viewpoint", which concerns the energic dimension of psychic phenomena. The economic viewpoint is one of the three aspects of Freud's metapsychology, alongside the dynamic and topographical viewpoints. In the dynamic aspect, psychic symptoms are considered to result from conflicts between psychic forces; the topographical aspect refers to a differentiation of the psychic apparatus in several different systems. The first topography distinguishes between the "unconscious, preconscious and conscious" systems; the second topography refers to three agencies–"the id, the ego and the superego". The economic viewpoint considers the destiny of the quantities of excitations that assail a human being in his daily life and assesses the nature of his cathexes in all his dimensions.

In privileging the economic aspect, with its energy requiring detailed study that is shared by the different organisational levels of the living being, I am postulating a distinction between somatic and libidinal energy. When libidinal energy loses its psychic quality during the somatisation process, it reverts into the somatic energy that conforms to the well-known laws of physicochemical processes.

The ensuing tensions and frustrations give rise to quantities of external and internal sensory excitations that, according to the Freudian model, impose a burden of work on the psychic apparatus, which in the most favourable case absorbs this quantity without any resulting imbalance. However, where malfunctions arise, as Marty's approach amply demonstrates, the psychic apparatus is flooded by the quantities of excitations and somatic disorders ensue.

The problem posed therefore concerns how this flooding, as yet unexplained, occurs: what becomes of this quantity of energy? By what processes is it transmitted?

I have tried to complete the developed model by introducing the concept of fluctuating impulses of psychic energy, which can be observed in clinical practice. It is possible to observe daily fluctuations in the libidinal and somatic tonus of patients who constantly confront us with oscillations in their condition. It has gradually become clear to me in the course of research that these impulses are transmitted from the psychic to the somatic sphere, gradually creating an imbalance in the homeostasis of the functions and organs.

When the psyche, which plays the primordial role in managing excitations, fails, *it is the body that takes over*.

The clinical and theoretical studies in this book are accompanied by some observations and investigations and in the final chapter I shall describe the psychotherapeutic approach to somatic patients. Through the example of a psychotherapy of a French-born patient of immigrant parents, I shall address a dimension that is rarely mentioned in psychotherapies, namely the importance of the cultural and anthropological component in human psychic and somatic functioning. All these observations will be addressed in accordance with the three above-mentioned dimensions: *the somatic, psychic and socio-cultural dimensions*.

CHAPTER ONE

Emotions and traumas

The desire to "heal" arose in that distant period of my childhood and in a sense I can say that in so far as possible I help to treat the "mind" of diseased bodies by incorporating in my therapeutic approach a consideration of the status of the illness from which patients are suffering, as well as the nature of the family and professional environment in which they are developing. Rather than taking the place of doctors who treat the body, I am exercising a complementary role that is necessary for returning to a form of mental functioning that is responsive to medical treatment. This consists in an inner mental attitude towards patients and their illnesses.

This attitude differs in certain respects from the perspective adopted by researchers and practitioners in various disciplines who operate within historically determined epistemological constraints and are accustomed to posing problems in a framework with which they are familiar, along the following lines:

- If the mind is disturbed (a disorder caused by multiple factors), it can generate somatic illnesses and the so-called psychosomatic and/or psychiatric approach is then required;

- If the body is ill and this involves some psychic disturbances, these are termed somatopsychic disorders;
- If the body and the mind are subject to disorders that both doctors and psychiatrists or psychoanalysts recognise as independent of each other, these would be treated separately.

My approach requires the use of concepts that provide a means of ascertaining pathways between these two entities that are the body and the mind. Progress in the neurosciences since the late 20th century and research conducted by some psychoanalysts have enabled me to outline the foundations of a comprehensive approach that takes account of the different organisational levels of the living being and to dispense with this model of the psyche-soma relationship, which leads to a methodological impasse.

I shall reiterate the three characteristics of the preliminary methodological approach: namely, *the somatic dimension, explained by the concept of somatic markers; the psychic dimension, explained by the existence of a coenaesthetic organisation connecting with somatic processes; and, finally, the socio-cultural dimension, which emphasises the characteristics of the 21st-century environment in determining the psychosexual maturation of individuals.*

This project is an endeavour to open the door that Freud closed nearly a century ago in order to be able to construct psychoanalysis; as he stated in a letter to Fliess dated September 22, 1898: "I am not at all in disagreement with you, not at all inclined to leave the psychology hanging in the air without an organic basis. But apart from this conviction I do not know how to go on, neither theoretically nor therapeutically and therefore must behave as if only the psychological were under consideration" (Freud to Fliess, 1985, p. 326).

Returning to childhood memories

One traumatic event often conceals another, in which case the emotion generated by the present-day event can reactivate a high-intensity emotional force connected with past events that then supplements the quantity of mental excitations, causing a flooding of psychic defences. I would like to discuss the occurrence of real events rather than fantasies that are, of course, closely connected with the emergence of these events.[5]

What might in fact have happened to my grandfather in an earlier period of his life? It suddenly comes back to me now that he was a wounded war veteran (First World War) and his left arm had been amputated. The loss of a limb and the inherent castration anxiety might have made him relive a painful and trying time that he never mentioned, at least in my presence, and that was never spoken of in the family ... I always thought that he was secretly suffering from this loss because it was impeding him in his daily life. However, I could not feel that this gave sufficient explanation of the somatisation process and his fragile condition; there had to be another factor. When I put some questions to my father, I learnt that two other events had taken place between seven and eight years before he died, which it seems to me had taken a constant and enduring toll on his psychic life: the disappearance of a sister of whom he was very fond and the implementation of the Vichy laws, with the appointment of an administrator for estates of which he was dispossessed. Being very young at this time, but aware of the vague threats that I was sensing in the company of the adults in the family, I knew that my grandfather had great difficulty tolerating these expropriations, which deprived him of economic means. The aspect that I will consider here is the temporal permanence of the emotional intensity and the traumatic experience of a man who bore considerable responsibility as the head of a very large family.

This return to a distant past set me wondering about the calm and serenity that imbued this man in the final moments of his life. How could this psychic recuperation be explained? It was then that I remembered that my grandmother had offered me the copies of the Bible and the Psalms that my grandfather had been reading. I had noticed some pencil markings that I had read without attaching any particular importance to them, but writing this book has led me to reconsider the problem. Why had he made these marks in the margins at certain paragraphs? What was he thinking about? Did he want to address a final message to the members of his family?

This is what I found: Deuteronomy 31, "Last words of Moses to all Israel". "I am an hundred and twenty years old this day; I can no more go out and come in: also the Lord hath said unto me, Thou shalt not go over this Jordan ... And the Lord said unto Moses, Behold, thy days approach that thou must die ... thou shalt sleep with thy fathers ... Yet thou shalt see the land before thee; but thou shalt not go thither unto the land which I give the children of Israel" (verses 2, 14, 16; Chapter 32, verse 52).

Even if his close family members were hiding the fatal outcome from him, my grandfather knew what he was dealing with. He knew that he was going to be taken away from the world of the living and he was struggling against this archaic anxiety by identifying with the fate of Moses, who knew that he was not going to cross over into Jordan because of his past sin and was worrying what would become of the people.

Similarly, my grandfather continued to worry about the future of his family and his children in the last few months of his life: were these sons going to follow in the footsteps of their ancestors? What would become of them?

Recourse to the spiritual life had procured for him a significant psychic recuperation that enabled him to confront his death.

I shall conclude this account by stating that the problem raised here is the destiny of anxiety and its somatic resonance,[6] namely the intense destructiveness engendered by the emotional burden and the constant pain. As a result of the trauma and constant stress, my grandfather was unable to elaborate psychically the large quantities of excitations that according to Freud's model were besieging him.

This deficiency, resulting from a momentary sideration of the psychic apparatus that facilitated the genesis of somatic illnesses, points to the existence in the nervous system of a preliminary sub-system consisting of emotions and behaviours. This sub-system is thus established in an early phase of the psychosexual maturation process. Damasio's contribution seems in many respects to provide the answer to my supposition.

Damasio's somatic markers

Communication between the levels of the living being involves discovery of the connections between emotions and physiological processes.

As Alexander had already observed: "The actual psychological content of an emotion must be studied with the most advanced methods of dynamic psychology and correlated with bodily responses" (1950, p. 11). To this, he added: "Emotional factors influence all body processes through nervous and humoral pathways" (p. 52).

This approach to the emotions is in fact one that has been taken since the earliest times. As William James observed: "What kind of an emotion of fear would be left if the feeling neither of quickened heart-beats nor of shallow breathing, neither of trembling lips nor of weakened limbs, neither of goose-flesh nor of visceral stirrings, were present, it is quite impossible for me to think" (1890, Vol. 2, p. 452). Our bodies thus express the entire gamut of our emotions through physiological processes but accordingly there is a wide range of stimuli and situations that are innate triggers of emotions connected with our past experiences.

This raises the question of how to establish if there is a phase of mental evaluation of the event before the emotion is triggered, conducted by intentional rather than automatic processes?

I do not advocate models of affectivity as such because we know that the problem is a more complex one, in that underneath the traumatic shock, the emotional onslaught and the repression of the accompanying affect the disorder is related to the repressed psychic representation. However, Damasio's research (1995) has led to the discovery of the neuronal circuit of emotions.

Primary emotions are innate and pre-programmed and they depend on neural circuits that form part of the limbic system; they do not account for the entire spectrum of emotional responses. It is these primary emotions that attract the attention of every observer of human nature and that were investigated by Hippocrates, Galen, Maimonides, William James and others, but these preliminary models do not provide an adequate description of all the body's responses to events.

According to Damasio, at the onset of a traumatic event a number of physiological modifications can be observed in the body: the heartbeat accelerates, the skin pales, the mouth dries, part of the intestines contracts, the back and neck muscles tense and, finally, the facial muscles take on a sad expression. Some changes therefore occur in the functioning of the viscera: the heart, lungs and intestines.

There are also some changes in the skin, the skeletal muscles and endocrine glands; finally, the immune system modifies–the tonus may either increase in the smooth muscles of the arterial walls, leading to a paling of the skin, or it may decrease, dilating the blood vessels, which produces a reddening of the skin. *This is how the home-ostasis of the organism is altered; it departs from the level of optimal average regulation.*

These bodily changes arise from thought processes consisting in mental representations[7] that are acquired in the course of development; these *acquired potential representations* contain the memory of the connections between emotions and situations as they have been experienced at the individual level. The circuit described by Damasio operates as follows: the acquired potential representations are localised in the frontal cortex and they engage the neural processes of the primary emotions, transmitting messages to the body via the peripheral nerves so that the viscera conform to the state generally associated with the type of situation that has triggered this entire process. Signals are transmitted to the motor system; the endocrine and nervous systems are activated, secreting hormones and peptides that produce changes in the states of the body and the brain; and, finally, the non-specific modulating neurones of the brain stem and the base of the telencephalon are activated, discharging their chemical messages to the basal ganglions and brain stem for example.

According to the above model, a specific event forms the object of a mental evaluation that generates responses emerging from potential representations that determine a bodily emotional state (information transmitted to the limbic and somatosensory systems). However, in addition to the bodily changes, the brain is operating in a continual perception of these bodily modifications. As human beings, we are continually receiving information about changes in the bodily state, from one second to the next, through *a neural loop working in parallel with a chemical loop*. It is the perception of what our body is doing while our thoughts unfold that we call "feeling an emotion". "In other words, a feeling depends on the juxtaposition of an image of the body proper to an image of something else, such as the visual image of a face or the auditory image of a melody" (Damasio, 1995, p. 145).

In conclusion, perceiving an emotion that relates to a particular phenomenon depends on the subjective quality of the perception of the phenomenon in question, the perception that this phenomenon engenders and the perception that all this brings to the tonality and efficacy of the thought processes. Although the body is the site of emotional expression, with the circuit running from the brain towards the body and back to the brain, in many cases the brain can create a bodily emotional state without having to reproduce it in the body. This suggests the likely hypothesis that the *processes of emotional simulation* are established during postnatal development while the organism is adapting to the environment. However, there are some differences between the bodily and mental reactions; like Damasio, I think that *the capacity to feel emotions entails the registration of bodily changes*. I should point out that other theorists take the view that changes in the bodily state arise in parallel with the perception of emotions rather than being the source. Accordingly, in any case, the perception is supplied by the process of simulation.

The work of Damasio and his team has demonstrated that, like the perception of any other image, the perception of emotions is a cognitive process."I do not see emotions and feelings as the intangible and vaporous qualities that many presume them to be. Their subject matter is concrete and they can be related to specific systems in body and brain, no less so than vision or speech". [1995, p. 164] The work of neuroscientists such as Edelman & Damasio provides sufficiently reliable hypotheses to help us to discover as yet little known processes of interrelation between mental, psychic and somatosensory functioning. In my view, Damasio provides us with one of the building blocks for establishing the connections with the structure of the perception-awareness-preconscious-unconscious system of Freud's first topography.

For Damasio, the somatic marker (1995) is *the association of a perception of an unpleasant or pleasant bodily sensation with a particular image (whether or not the perception is visceral in origin) as a decision is being taken*. The somatic marker acts either as an alarm signal–the danger of choosing this solution–or as an encouraging signal; in either case, it is a system that provides indications as to direction. It therefore appears that in addition to the neuronal processes that subtend the primary emotions, allowing many situations and adapted somatic states to be paired, some somatic markers are acquired during childhood and adolescence. This marking is a continual process that ceases only on death. The markers are acquired under the auspices of an internal homeostatic system that strives to ensure the organism's survival. "The internal preference system is inherently biased to avoid pain, seek potential pleasure and is probably pretuned for achieving these goals in social situations" (p. 179).[8]

The concept of the "somatic marker" constitutes an important contribution to progress in the neurosciences and provides us with the elements that point to the existence of an emotional and behavioural neuronal sub-system, a non-verbal and unconscious organisation.

These elements that encode the sensory, motor and emotional experience of the body thus facilitate the creation of an organisation of the psychic apparatus.

By what processes does this take place? This is the next question that I shall be addressing while considering the emergence of the psychic apparatus within the bounds of the living being's "material organisation".

Somatopsychic organisations

We could reply to this question by turning to René Spitz's remarkable study, *The First Year of Life* (1965). Writers and researchers who refer to Spitz tend to quote the anxiety of the eighth month of life as the organiser of the psyche. This corresponds to a more advanced developmental stage of the psychic organisation. This anxiety at eight months of age demonstrates that the child "has now established a true object relation and that the mother has become his libidinal object, his love object" (1965, p. 156).[9] Now, our research is concerned with an earlier developmental stage, namely the first few weeks of life.

Spitz uses this model of the psychic organiser to explain the apprehension of phenomena relating to the integration and constitution of the psyche. Three independent developmental trends combine to bring about the construction of the child's personality through the constitution of the libidinal object: "The crystallization of affective response, the integration of the ego and the consolidation of object relations" (1965, p. 161). The first somatopsychic organisation according to this hypothesis is that which Spitz terms a *coenaesthetic organisation or system.*

According to Spitz, human beings have a system of "feeling" from birth that differs from the familiar adult perceptual system that only comes into operation later. The somatic dimension of this specific organisation is principally visceral, based in the autonomic nervous system, and it reveals itself in the form of emotional manifestations. This is a process of "reception"; the visceral sensitivity is connected with certain sensory zones such as the surface of the skin. There are also certain sensory zones and organs that can be considered as transitional, which play an intermediary role between the peripheral and visceral sensory organs, between external and internal. Among these transitional organs, Spitz mentions: the larynx, the pharynx, the tongue, the inside of the cheeks and the lips; the chin, nose and cheeks and the inner ear. These organs mediate between internal reception and external perception and each of them has important survival function in the alimentary process. They have a supportive function and underpin the transition between coenaesthetic reception and diacritical perception. Spitz emphasises that "much as the coenesthetic organization has become muted in the consciousness of Western man, it continues to function covertly" (p. 45). This organisation plays a fundamental role in our feelings, thoughts and actions; according to Spitz, we are accustomed to thinking in terms of the unconscious when it is the characteristics of the coenaesthetic organisation that are in operation.

The second somatopsychic organisation or *diacritic organisation* allows the following somatic changes to be ascertained: "The myelinization of neural pathways is now sufficiently advanced to make the diacritic functioning of the sensory apparatus possible; to achieve coordination of the effectors; to place groups of skeletal muscles in the service of directed action sequences; and to permit adjustments of posture and equilibrium which serve as the basis for muscular action ... an increasing number of memory traces has been stored, so that mental operations of growing complexity can be carried out ... *in the psychic organization,* maturation and development of the congenital equipment have made it possible to place the effectors in the service of sequences of directed actions. These action sequences permit the infant to discharge affective tension in an intentional, directed manner, that is, volitionally" (1965, p. 162).

The second organiser or diacritical organisation forms an indispensable link in the somatopsychic continuum; the diacritical organisation stems from the coenaesthetic organisation and the two organisations are in constant communication.

> The coenaesthetic organization continues to function throughout life, powerfully one might say, as the wellspring of life itself, even though our Western civilization has fitted a silencer on its manifestations. In emergencies, under stress, the archaic forces sweep the silencer away and break through with terrifying violence, for they are not under rational conscious control. Then we are confronted with the more or less random explosive discharge of primal emotions, with malignant psychosomatic disease, or with certain forms of psychotic outbreaks. [1965, pp. 45–6]

The coenaesthetic and diacritic organisations coexist in the same organism but are radically different. In psychoanalytic terms, Spitz compares the relationship between the coenaesthetic and diacritical organisations to the relationship between the primary and secondary processes: "We mostly become aware of the muted operations of the coenaesthetic system either through the distortions it imposes upon diacritic functioning or through its influence on the primary process" (p. 134). With the appearance of the smile (third month) the mnemonic traces are established, which means that the constituent parts of the psychic apparatus are in place: conscious, preconscious, unconscious (Freud's first topography). A rudimentary ego develops within the somatopsychic continuum, which displays increasingly coordinated and directed muscular activity; Freud (1923) termed this first nucleus of the ego *the body ego*.

Spitz locates the formation of the bodily ego at an earlier age than Glover (1956), namely at three months, such that: "The prototypes of psychic ego nuclei are to be found in physiological functions and somatic behavior" (pp. 103–4). The somatic barrier that functions from birth to protect against stimuli is then gradually replaced by a more efficient and more integrated organisation that operates selectively; the energic charges brought by the stimuli are distributed between the various systems of mnemonic traces and are either kept in reserve or discharged in the form of directed actions. Accordingly, the directed action becomes an outlet for the discharge of libidinal and aggressive energy, accelerating the development of the psychic apparatus.

The transition is thus made from a somatic mode to a psychic mode of energy discharge. Damasio's somatic markers thus represent the constituent elements of the neuronal and biological foundations of the coenaesthetic organisation described by Spitz. The contributions of these two researchers converge, establishing the building blocks for connections between somatic and psychic functions. Spitz helps us to situate this organisation in time; that is, in the pre-objectal period that is dominated by the primary process, non-fusion of the drives and the cathexis of libidinal energy. This therefore occurs within the bounds of several levels of the living being.

It is this organisation that manifests itself, in my view, in regressions or disorganisations of the psychic apparatus.[10]

The discharge of tensions produced by (internal and external) sensory stimuli becomes more specific with the establishment of the libidinal object (mother), through the processes of gradual integration of the somatic functions and development of the psychic functions (somatic markers and coenaesthetic organisation). The development of a psychic apparatus then allows a more harmonious and more diversified functioning of the discharge of tensions: affective and behavioural expressions, followed by verbal manifestations and secondary processes; that is, the constitution of the pre-conscious that assists the binding of drive forces expressed at the (unconscious) primary-process level with the representations localised in the preconscious (secondary process). The role played by the two drives (aggressive and libidinal) is fundamental in the integration, coordination and structuring of the ego. The sexual and aggressive drives are progressively fused throughout the process of psychosexual maturation by the introjection of the object. This reconsideration of drive development raises some questions about the malfunctioning of the two drives and the destiny of the energy.

For both Freud and Spitz, the muscular apparatus is the privileged channel of discharge for the aggressive drive and seems to predominate from birth (the immediate discharges thus preventing unpleasure) but Freud developed a theory concerning the affinity of the libidinal drive for the viscera. The organ systems are infinitely slower than the skeletal musculature in discharge; it seems that the viscera have the capacity to retain bound energy, which is not the case for the other route, which discharges energy rapidly in short bursts of pressure.

Freud's exposition gives us a better understanding of how in psychic regressions or disorganisations the libidinal drive, defused from the aggressive drive, has the choice between an immediate discharge through the motor route or a slower discharge through the visceral route.

The psychic apparatus therefore emerges at the crossroads of many somatic functions and constitutes an indispensable element of the general equilibrium of a human being in all his dimensions. The complex apparatus that is the product of psychosexual development emerges in a familial, socio-cultural, economic and political environment. The maturation of the psychic apparatus and its establishment in definitive form depend heavily on the space and time of its genesis. Its relative resistance or fragility is determined by the combination of the genetic inheritance and events in the environment. Let us now examine this dimension.

The political, economic and socio-cultural environment of the 20ᵗʰ century: psychic and somatic disorders

During the 20ᵗʰ century, the globalisation of warfare, the mass destruction of populations and nations, decolonisation, the Nazi and other totalitarian regimes, transcontinental migration, changing socio-cultural value systems in western countries and their gradual propagation in continents unprepared or ill-prepared to adopt them, the increasing pace of technological advance and so on have created a new environment for humanity that is principally characterised by day-to-day violence. More than in other historical periods, human beings are subjected to major or minor traumas throughout their family and professional lives and strong demands are made on their mental and biological defences. Human beings are confronted on a daily and continual basis with major or minor stresses. This new environment has substantially modified and weakened the biological and psychic functioning of humanity.

Despite their differences of approach, medical and psychoanalytic theorists and practitioners of psychosomatics are agreed on the factors that give rise to somatic diseases; their view is shared by the proponents of the stress-based approach. However, they do not draw the same conclusions; some refer to the flooding of the psychic apparatus by the quantity of excitations generated by trauma, using Freud's first topographical model (unconscious-preconscious-conscious), while others link the discharge of excitations in the body with adaptational illnesses caused by stress; this latter approach privileges the somatic dimension and downplays the psychological dimension. However, recently a more comprehensive approach has emerged, namely the *psychobiological* approach, which seeks to ascertain the interactions between the nervous system, the endocrine system, the immune system, behaviours and emotions and so on that produce physiological or biochemical changes in living organisms (Rossi, 1993).

The explanatory hypothesis of somatisation processes common to all these approaches has been extremely well formulated by Pierre Marty, who summarises it as follows: "Somatic diseases generally stem from the individual's inadequacies with regard to the living conditions that he encounters". Marty is referring here to traumatic events, since according to psychosomatic theoretical hypotheses, "when the combined availability of the mental apparatus and the behavioural systems is superseded or rendered inoperative by a new situation, it is the somatic apparatus that responds" (1990, p. 48).

What is the nature of these "new situations?" What are these traumatic events? In 1967 in the *Journal of Psychosomatic Research*, Holmes and Rahe established a scale of 43 items representing family, personal and professional situations with economic, financial, social and other dimensions that forced individuals to adapt to changes. These two researchers developed their scale based on interviews with 2000 employees of the American Navy, who described changes that had occurred in their personal and family lives over the previous ten years.

In his work *La Psychosomatique de l'Adulte* (1990), Marty also gave some examples of traumas: losing a loved one, a professional or family role, a friendship or sexual relationship, a group to which one belongs, but also the loss of an earlier way of life, a particular freedom, a physiological function (menopause, amputation etc.) or a mental function, for example in ageing, a loss of sexual functioning, a sports activity, a work project or holiday plans, but also losing a fantasmatic representation during one of the above losses.

The relationship between traumatic events and the stress they produce has been the object of many epidemiological studies (Stora, 2005). Every change makes strong demands on the human capacity for psychic and somatic adaptation. Social mobility and migration are considered to be factors that cause mental illnesses and somatic disorders. It has thus been demonstrated that emigrant populations have higher hospitalisation rates than other groups in the population. The factors that account for this psychic fragility are cultural differences–between the culture of origin and the country of adoption–the economic and social conditions of the new society and the exertions made towards assimilation by the emigrant populations.

Vulnerability to somatic diseases, as opposed to psychic disorders, has also been studied; Graham (1945) demonstrates that geographically mobile men have higher rates of coronary disease than those who are geographically stable. The Irish who emigrated to the United States at the beginning of the 20th century had higher rates of tuberculosis than their compatriots who remained in the country, despite the fact that their standard of living was very generally higher. Rapid industrialisation and urban reconstruction have a debilitating impact on individuals. The first generation of peasants or mountain-dwellers who worked in industrial sectors in cities suffered from more somatic disorders than their descendants who were employed in the same factories. We also know that when economic activity declines, the general level of social stress increases in conjunction with hospitalisation for mental disorders. When psychosexual stress manifests itself, the cohesion of the social group, acting as an emotional shock absorber or maternal protective barrier, plays an important role in preventing hospitalisation, as was demonstrated by a survey of admission rates to New York State Hospital over a period of one hundred and twenty years.

In the course of my hospital experience, I encountered a large number of patients who bore witness to this lack of community support, having suffered accidents during debilitating periods of their lives. I often wondered about the impact of their living conditions on their health and their capacity, following treatment, to resume their activities, while the economic, social, professional and family circumstances had remained unaltered.

Traumatic factors such as natural disasters, civil wars, deportations, uprooting of populations can involve the disintegration and disorganisation of entire communities (e.g. Lebanon in 1989 or Rwanda). All the studies point to an increase in mental disorders, tuberculosis, heart attacks and hypertension that accompanies events of this kind, which points to the conclusion that *the absence and the disintegration of social structures weaken the individual's mental and biological defences.* Many pathological manifestations of traumatic origin occur in exceptional events (other than wars) caused by technological civilisation or natural disasters that assume vast proportions because of urban development: rail accidents, shipwrecks, fires, earthquakes, hurricanes, volcanic eruptions, floods, accidents at nuclear power stations (Chernobyl, Three Mile Island). The exceptional events in our contemporary world include the trauma of rape, the syndrome of the prisoner-of-war, concentration camps, hostages (in aeroplane hijackings, bank robberies or embassies–Peru 1997).

Many authors have emphasised the *latency period* between the traumatic event and the onset of psychic and/or somatic pathologies. They all agree on the following sequence: an impact phase of shock and sideration; a phase of inhibition and denial; a phase of repetitive intrusions; a progressive recovery phase; a phase of acceptance in which the traumatic event begins to be integrated and there are some amnesic residues (Rivolier, 1989).

Contemporary history, dominated by the speed of technological advance, economic globalisation, urban violence and international and regional wars has thus, among other factors, *generated new forms of structure in the human psyche.* Contemporary psychic structures are therefore different from those still described in our day by certain psychoanalysts who continue to talk about classical analysis (classical neuroses: obsessional, phobic, hysterical), although these patients now represent only around five percent of the psychotherapeutic treatments in present-day clinical practice. *It goes without saying that the sector of the population in Vienna at the beginning of the 20th century, highlighted by Sigmund Freud, can no longer constitute a representative sample of our studies at the beginning of the 21st century.*

These observations do not challenge Freud's model of psychic functioning but seek to place it in a contemporary scientific perspective. Obsessional and phobic neuroses belong to the traditional terrain of psychoanalysis and still constitute one of the extremes on the spectrum of psychic functioning; *by contrast, behavioural and character neuroses involve "most of the populations of our time and region"* (Marty, 1976, p. 113).

Freud considered traumatic neurosis to be a metapsychological exception; with Sara & César Botella (1992) of the Paris Psychoanalytical Society, I take the view that, without contradicting Freud's notion, traumatic neurosis is best understood not as a metapsychological model in itself, less still a model that can be opposed to psychoneurosis, but as something that *"belongs to the realm of a potentiality that exists in all structures, including the best mentalised and not that of a sort of failure or ... something resulting from a moment of psychic disturbance"* (1992, p. 25).

I am referring here not only to the isolated and violent trauma with an intrusive force but also to the trauma of indeterminate duration that can accompany human lives at the individual and collective level for months or even years, which according to my hypothesis involves constant stress. To understand the clinical profile of *contemporary present-day neuroses*, we must think in terms of a treatment for trauma and constant stress. This treatment has gradually been developed since the end of the Second World War by Marty and the members of the Paris School of Psychosomatics, some psychoanalysts from the Paris Psychoanalytical Society (the work of the negative, the mechanism of foreclosure or repudiation), some psychoanalysts from other schools (Guir, 1983) and by Peter Sifneos in Boston, as well as researchers in the neurosciences, whose studies of the neural processes of perception have made a substantial contribution to elucidating the problem. We have reached the beginning of the 21st century with a theoretical corpus and a clinical practice that are better adapted to human therapeutic needs.

A traumatic event can be a factor that triggers an imbalance leading to psychic and somatic disorders, according to the multifactorial and multi-causal model (Engel, 1977) that I have adopted from the outset of this exposition. The clinical approach now leads us to assess the consequences of such an event at the collective level and its repercussions at the individual psychic and somatic level. In other words, where large quantities of excitations flood the mental apparatus, *the coenaesthetic organisation and the somatic markers of bioregulation take over*.

These excitational discharges and flows are drained by the libidinal and somatic energy–what are the mechanisms and laws that govern these processes? This is what I shall be studying in the next chapter in order to complete the theoretical outline before embarking on the presentation of clinical investigations in the chapters that follow.

CHAPTER TWO

The economic viewpoint and mentalisation processes

"Clinical observation slowly taught me that all analysands (and analysts as well) somatize at one time or another, particularly when stressful events override their usual ways of dealing with mental pain and conflict".

[Joyce McDougall, *Theaters of the Body* 1989, p. 20]

The role of psychic energy in somatisation processes

The strange death of Mrs S—cardiac impulses and turbulence. It is well-known how vulnerable cardiac patients can be to their emotions: I shall begin by reporting a case that unfolded in a hospital department in Boston in the United States. This concept of vulnerability[11] is an important one to take into account because some patients seem to become more vulnerable in a hospital setting; in fact, patients cathect their illnesses and their organs or functions in highly specific ways. They are usually completely unaware of the full diagnostic picture and they lack authority in relation to the doctors who are tending them, despite the fact that it is their bodies that are calling for attention and are receiving all the care. In a situation of this kind, patients are highly sensitive to verbal and non-verbal cues from doctors for a wide range of reasons. These signals can either boost their healing capacities or exacerbate their illnesses, particularly if the doctor is not well informed as to the possible effects of his behaviour on his patients.

Having made these preliminary remarks, I should now like to move on to the observation made in 1965 by Dr Bernard Lown, a famous cardiologist who was confronted with a tragic situation as a young intern when he was treating some patients in the department of Dr S. A. Levine, a professor of cardiology at Harvard Medical School. He described Professor Levine as a perceptive observer who formulated precise diagnoses and had an astounding memory, as well as an outstanding clinician who had the confidence of the patients in his care. During a visit to one of the hospital departments where the intern was practising, Professor Levine examined one of the patients being treated by the young intern. She was suffering from a heart disease (contraction of the right heart valve, the tricuspid valve); this middle-aged patient was a librarian whom Levine had treated in the past. On entering the room, he greeted her very warmly and, turning towards the non-residential medical students and clinical directors who were attending the interview, he said to them, "This woman has a TS" and, as he was pressed for time, he quickly left the room. As soon as Professor Levine went away, the patient's behaviour changed; she became anxious and frightened and her pulse accelerated to 150 beats per minute; she was sweating and she then suffered a massive pulmonary oedema. The intern asked her why she was feeling so anxious and the patient replied that Professor Levine had told her that she was in a "TS"–that is to say, a "terminal situation". Now, in using the initials "TS", Levine had in fact meant "Tricuspid stenosis" (stenosis of the tricuspid valve). Despite all the treatment that was given in order to reverse the dying process and the intern's strenuous efforts to reassure the patient, as well as the endeavours to find Professor Levine, Mrs S died later that same day (it had been impossible to reverse the process of flooding from a massive pulmonary oedema) (Kabat-Zin, 1990).[12]

In this highly dramatic incident, we have a demonstration of the anxiety provoked by a quantity of excitations that Mrs S was unable to master, revealing a state of distress; this could not be eliminated by the process of psychic work that was quickly overwhelmed–as

Freud states: "One can save oneself from an external danger by flight; fleeing from an internal danger is a difficult enterprise" (1933, p. 84). I think that in this case the mental elaboration of an emotional surge (which can be considered as an extremely intense stress) was rendered impossible by the rapidity with which the excitations spread through the apparatuses. I should emphasise a point that is often underestimated, namely that *the onset and implementation of the work of mental elaboration are protracted processes.*

It will thus be understood that the psychic apparatus is temporarily sidelined and that the excitations transmitted by the impulse of libidinal energy that returns to the self, to primary narcissism, with a view to protecting life, cannot stop the flooding and that the impulse continues to be inexorably transmitted in milliseconds to the diseased organ, in this case the heart. The path was already completely cleared because this organ had been diseased for a very long time; the concept of somatic compliance (Freud), as well as somatic vulnerability, finds an application here. In this specific case, both the psychic defence mechanisms and the biological regulators of the cardiac function were bypassed. Flooded by the energy stored by the emotional surge, the homeostatic mechanisms that must provide cardiac equilibrium malfunctioned under the impact of a reaction to a stress of the greatest possible intensity.

The understanding of somatisation processes–that is, the emergence of illnesses–is based, in my hypothesis, on the fluctuations and oscillations of energy caused by emotional turmoil associated with traumatic events, whether these are isolated or constant in duration, transmitted by somatic markers and the coenaesthetic somatopsychic organisation to all the bodily functions and organs.

The notions of energy move into the foreground when we examine the biological phenomena: from this perspective, all manifestations of life are based on a complicated series of chemical and physical processes occurring in the metabolism. These notions were an influence on Freud's idea of tracing the destiny of quantities of excitation and reaching at least some relative estimates of their size. This is what he terms "the economic point of view" (Laplanche & Pontalis, 1973, p. 127), which he examined in *Studies on Hysteria* (1893–95), then in the works on mourning, narcissistic neuroses (the notion of a balance of energy between the subject's various cathexes), traumatic neuroses (disorders caused by an excessively intense shock) and so on. The economic viewpoint is the essential driving principle of *the psychic apparatus, which accomplishes a fundamental work of maintaining at its lowest possible level the energy that circulates there, transforms the free energy (primary process) into bound energy (secondary process), defers discharge and elaborates excitations; this apparatus receives excitations of both external and internal origin.* Internal bodily excitations are the sources of the drives, exerting a constant pressure that imposes a burden of work on the psyche.

The constancy principle regulates the functioning of the psychic apparatus, namely to maintain constancy in the sum of excitations by activating avoidance mechanisms in response to external excitations and discharge mechanisms in response to internal excitations. This constancy principle can be explained in terms of thermodynamic laws as a closed system (Carnot's second principle of thermodynamics); in fact, organisms are constantly exchanging matter and energy (exergonic reactions leading to low-energy states and endergonic reactions, in which the reverse process occurs).

The constancy principle has also been defined as the maintenance of a constant level in the sum of energies in a closed system, or with reference to the physiologist Cannon (1914) as the maintenance of a constant level of energy with regard to the external environment, a notion of constancy that is similar to the notion of homeostasis.[13]

In summary, with regard to a "quantum"[14] (quantity) of internal or external excitations, the functioning of the Freudian model offers the following possibilities:

1. discharge via motricity (behaviours accompanied by affects, based on sensorimotor activity, which may or may not be connected with more or less elaborated mental representations). Behaviours can cover the entire expressive range from thing-representations (unrepresentable material) to elaborated mental representations; behaviours can serve as a temporary discharge of external and internal excitations;

2. somatic conversion: "In hysteria, the incompatible idea is rendered innocuous by *its sum of excitation* being *transformed into something somatic.* For this I should like to propose the name of *conversion*" (Freud, 1894, p. 49). The psychic outlet in the body is made possible by somatic compliance, resulting from the

impossibility of affect discharge and the repression of mental representations. In this case, it is a problematic that belongs to the secondary process, thus energy connected with representations;

3. the somatic excitation (Freud postulates a somatic sexual excitation) is transformed into a psychic excitation, which eliminates the existing somatic excitation. This "quantum" of excitation can precipitate an anxiety attack and, confronted with the danger of a dreaded satisfaction of the drive movement, the ego instigates the automatism of the pleasure-unpleasure principle, which represses the dangerous drive movement. "The more the generation of anxiety can be restricted to a mere signal, so much the more does the ego expend on actions of defence which amount to the psychical binding of the repressed [impulse] and so much the closer, too, does the process approximate to a normal working-over of it, though no doubt without attaining to it" (Freud, 1933, p. 90).

4. the "quantum" of excitation is taken up by an external figure (the mother or her substitute); this intervention of protective shields makes it possible to stop the discharge of excitations inside the body, enabling the baby and young child to resume a satisfactory somatic and psychic functioning. In truth, this specific mode of discharge described by Freud can be rediscovered throughout adult life, since this type of recourse seeks to diminish or eliminate excitations (family life, friendships, psychotherapy, medication etc.).

Freud's model of the destiny of the "quantum" of excitations can be considered as a model of the functioning of a *psychic apparatus envisaged as a closed system* that is dynamic but that regardless of the magnitude of the drive impulses returns to a state of equilibrium, which is facilitated by psychic defence mechanisms. I should also emphasise *mutatis mutandis* that Freud hypothesises a fully constituted psychic apparatus for all individuals at the end of the psychosexual maturation process.

These two statements concerning the nature of the system—a closed system—and the nature of psychic structuring have been challenged by scientific advances that consider organisms as open systems that are continually exchanging matter, energy or information with their environment.

This dynamic equilibrium in an open system is termed *flux-equilibrium* (Bertallanfy, 1968), a concept that applies not only to biological phenomena but also in the domain of physics (watercourses), chemistry (flames), ecology, politics and economics. In the realm of mental structures, as we will see below, under the combined influence of the socio-cultural and familial environment, we are confronted with new mental structurings. In this new frame of reference, what happens to the economic viewpoint and its functional processes?

I recall that for Freud libidinal energy has a somatic and sexual source with which it is nevertheless not identical; it "could serve as a measure of processes and transformations occurring in the field of sexual excitation" and its "production, increase or diminution, distribution and displacement should afford us possibilities for explaining the psychosexual phenomena observed" (1905, p. 217). "We distinguish this libido in respect of its special origin from the energy which must be supposed to underlie mental processes in general and we thus also attribute a *qualitative* character to it" (p. 217).

During traumas and constant stress, the libido loses its characteristic qualities by converting back into the somatic energy that fuels the life processes; in the process, it becomes the object of substantial variations and fluctuations that disturb the homeostasis.

However, before it loses its psychic characteristics, clinical observation reveals to us the highs and lows, in other words the fluctuations of this energy. What are the explanatory models for these phenomena?

In modern biological theory, living organisms are dynamic, complex open systems that are dissipative and unstable. Whereas the dynamic equilibrium in a closed system is inherently reversible because the opposed processes–construction and deterioration–occur simultaneously, the flux equilibrium in an open system is irreversible. As concerns the above-mentioned second principle of thermodynamics, in its usual form it is not applicable to open systems.

The laws that apply there are probabilistic in nature since, as Prigogine and Stengers (1984) demonstrate, all deterministic theories inevitably based on the necessary sequence of cause and effect are gradually being replaced by statistics. They define what they term *dissipative structures*: chemical reactions, for example, in conditions of non-equilibrium can engender the spontaneous appearance of structures that show a degree of order. *A particular system can thus contain more than one stable solution* and, according to the type of random disturbance in the system at the moment that it becomes unstable, one or other type of organisation appears. The system then develops through a series of random disturbances (chaos theory) and the emergence of new organisations.

According to Prigogine and Stengers (1984), these new stable states (order) that emerge from random disturbances (chaotic states) are most characteristic of modern science and are valid for all disciplines. *In summary, systems can have average behaviours that fluctuate within certain limits over a very long period and then, undergoing an external disturbance, the system can establish itself in another behaviour that still fluctuates, but around another mean.*

Most natural phenomena, like those in physics, are governed by laws that are simultaneously dynamic and non-linear. Everything is ordered by relations that exist in a temporal sequence and interact with each other. According to Prigogine and Stengers, the complexity and unpredictability of these physical phenomena are the same in nature as those that are observable in social organisations and living organisms.

These observations by a specialist in dissipative energy systems tie in with our investigations into somatic energy since the outset of this chapter, because by virtue of belonging to living organisms it partakes of these laws of energy, which therefore enables us to gain an understanding of its fluctuations and the observable presence of various stable states that arise from disease-generated disturbances.

The subjective nature of human beings introduces a qualitative dimension that we can only comprehend by means of these quantitative models, which then provide us by analogy with the necessary metaphors for understanding how energy processes unfold in the sphere of the psychic apparatus. We are all highly conscious of this when, as psychoanalysts, we refer to libidinal impulses and fluctuations, processes of displacement, cathexis and decathexis and even libidinal haemorrhage.

Moreover, these theories seem to share the same kind of investigation in terms of our clinical practice: what was the state of the patient's system or equilibrium at the outset? This problem was formulated by Edward Lorenz (1963), who was interested in the problem of atmospheric "convection"; minor variations in certain variables in a non-linear dynamic system can initially have vast totally unforeseen consequences. The evolution over time depends on what is known as *sensitive dependence on the initial conditions*.

Does the same apply to psychic structures? In fact, we know nothing about the initial conditions of these systems; we can only observe them at the manifestation of unstable states.

In many disciplines–such as biology, demography, cosmology and information technology–researchers accept and recognise the chaotic nature of these systems. However, in the case of dissipative systems–that is, systems that dissipate their energies externally, *there emerge pockets of stability, regularity and order, known as "strange attractors"*. Just like the drainage basins of rivers, over the long term attractors represent the only possible forms of behaviour for a complex system. In the short term, every point of the phase space can represent a possible behaviour of a dynamic system. What do we mean by the term "phase space"? Transitional phases are familiar from animal locomotion; when a horse gains speed, it moves from a walk to a trot and then to a gallop in order to minimise the expenditure of energy. It is consequently possible to have several viable types of functioning in these organisations, the equilibrium of which corresponds to the dynamics and the pressures of the time; in the worst case, this can be a mortal stability–that is to say, a disorganisation, when the living creature or organisation or human society, as a result of the internal and external forces at work, is led to disintegration and sometimes to death. *"In the short term any point in phase space can stand for a possible behavior of the dynamical system. In the long term the only possible behaviors are the attractors themselves.* Other kinds of motion are transient. *By definition, attractors have the important property of stability"* (Gleick, 1988, p. 138, my italics).

These basins of energy attraction constitute a very striking image of stable states within a larger whole that is dominated by instability; this metaphor of the collection of fluids demarcates a space of psychic functioning in which a degree of stability manifests itself, a space that is determined by the individual's personal history.

This is my experience of the study of economic systems and their short-term cycles, which encourages me to state that initially researchers find stability and determinism in a universe that they implicitly suppose to be constant and long-term, whereas in fact it is instability that prevails.

These considerations have taken us a long way from the tragic case of Mrs S in Boston. The human body is the prime example of an unstable complex system; physiological researchers, who regarded the organ of the heart as the seat of impulses and oscillations, used the mathematical model of chaos theory. They are seeking to develop a general approach to the heart's functioning; the various parts of a heart in fibrillation seem to function, whereas the whole reveals disorder. Fibrillation is a disorder in a complex system and does not disappear of its own accord, since this form of chaos is stable. Only an electrical discharge, equivalent to a huge disturbance, can return the heart to a steady state. Defibrillators are generally effective, but without a clear understanding of the dynamics of the heart it is impossible to predict the outcome caused by its use, particularly when there are multiple disturbances, as was the case with this patient, who initially suffered a major psychic disturbance. These disturbances introduce into the complex dynamic system a series of contingencies, of which no one truly knows the outcome. With reference to this problem of pathologies that conform to "non-periodic" laws, Professor David Ruelle (1991) has observed that although normal cardiac regulation is periodic there are many non-periodic pathologies (such as ventricular fibrillation) that lead to the state of equilibrium consisting in death. It appears that great medical benefits might be drawn from computer studies of a realistic mathematical model that would reproduce the various dynamic systems of the heart.

On an experimental basis, I am presenting a mathematical model that refers to chaos theory (see Appendix 2); this is a simplified explanatory model of fluctuations in psychic energy according to the quantity of endogenous and exogenous excitations induced by a traumatic event. This model uses the concept of mentalisation developed by Pierre Marty (1976, 1980), a key concept of the psychic structure in the explanation of somatisation processes.

Mentalisations and somatisation processes

The model that Pierre Marty (founder of what is known as the Paris School and the Institute of Psychosomatics) developed from Freud's model is based on the recognition of differences in individual psychic structuring, mainly due to education, which affect the constitution of the psychic apparatus; these developmental contingencies hinder the establishment of the various mental organisations and sometimes result in the malfunctioning or inaccessibility of the psychic apparatus. This psychosomatic theory is characterised by formulating a structure that links somatic and psychic functions throughout the maturational process under the influence of *individual life impulses*. To return to Freud's model, the "quantum" of excitations imposes a burden of work on the psychic apparatus, binding the free energy of primary processes with mental word-representations from the secondary processes (bound energy). This binding operation constitutes the work of mental elaboration. In fact, this binding is only possible if these representations are accessible. What happens to this in the alternative case?

Based on extensive clinical experience, in 1975 Pierre Marty developed the concept of mentalisation with reference to the quantity and quality of psychic representations in individuals. The representations constitute the foundation of mental life; this is composed of thing-representations (of a sensorimotor order) and behaviours associated or otherwise, as well as affects belonging to the primary processes and therefore belongs to the unconscious. The binding of thing-representations and word-representations emerges from communications between child, mother, father and the family environment and this constitutes the essential foundation of associative chains of ideas. The accumulation of representations throughout the maturational process will determine their quantity. Marty uses the metaphor of layers of representations to indicate their temporal stratification and their quality consists in: 1. their accessibility to recall; 2. the accessibility, during their recall, of their bindings to other representations from the same or different periods, all of which combined allow the richness of mental life to be assessed; 3. the constancy of these accessibilities. The constancy can either be temporarily interrupted or compromised by the avoidance or suppression of representations, or again by disorganisations of the preconscious system. The preconscious system, the psychic organisation of Freud's first topography, is the site of the binding of word-representations and thing-representations and, in consequence, *the hub of the psychosomatic economy.*

I should state that the concept of the richness of mental representations is still highly subjective and, clinically, it varies considerably according to the individual concerned and his familial, social, cultural and professional status; there does not yet exist any relative scale of comparison, hence the difficulty of assessing this density of the preconscious. In order to do this, psychosomaticians work from the basis of their clinical experience, which is of course restricted to certain social environments and often contains an ethnic bias. Many psychologists, psychoanalysts, psychosomaticians and others use the concepts of hyposymbolisation and imaginative deficiency to attempt to determine this clinical phenomenon from the observation of somatic patients (Haynal & Pasini, 1978; Sami-Ali, 1987).

Marty's idea, following Freud, was to demonstrate that in the work of mental elaboration, external and internal excitations are gradually absorbed by the stratified layers accumulated over time as they become connected with representations. It is in fact possible to assess the existence of associative chains in the present and the journeys back and forth between present and past more easily and intuitively in clinical work. I have often observed in my clinical work, as Marty put it, a temporary inaccessibility of representations in patients, as a sign of temporary or more severe and disorganising disorders. Although I think that this notion requires further development, its clinical and theoretical utility is undeniable.

Marty's economic viewpoint is based on criteria of good and poor mentalisation to explain the somatisation processes. 1. When mentalisation is good and instinctual and drive-based excitations are of average size (average accumulation), we observe the emergence of somatic complaints that are usually spontaneously reversible. Marty refers to functionally localisable, non-progressive complaints that are non-life-threatening: asthma, eczema, gastritis, ulcers, rachialgia, cephalalgia, migraines. 2. When the excitations are great and accumulate in subjects with poor mentalisation, we observe the emergence of severe and progressive somatic complaints: cardio-vascular diseases, auto-immune diseases, cancers, or any life-threatening illness (Marty, 1991).

We can summarise below the progress of the two principal somatisation processes (Stora, 1994, 1995, 1996). This summary is taken from a publication in the *Annales de Psychiatrie*. It is the product of some extensive research that Marty and I conducted in our application of the psychosomatic classification that he created, which I continued to develop after his death in 1993 until 2005 (version 5 of the classification):

Progress of Reversible Somatisations

First stage. Excessive excitations, average accumulation;

Second stage. Slight mental disorganisation, accompanied by acute or subacute depression;

Third stage. Psychic regression, increase in anxieties, onset of various (e.g. phobic) symptoms, as well as characterological or behavioural symptoms;

Fourth stage. First fairly unremarkable somatic disorganisation;

Fifth stage. Emergence of the somatic complaint;

Sixth stage. End of the disorganising impulse.

Progress of Severe Somatisations

First stage. Large accumulations of excitations; no possibility of mental elaboration; reduced possibilities of outflow into behaviours;

Second stage. Mental disorganisation according to the quantity and quality of mental representations;

Third stage. Essential depression, resumption of a childhood depression or more pronounced resumption of a latent depression;

Fourth stage. Emergence of diffuse anxieties, symptom of a state of distress, absence of psychic regression; mental life is reduced to thing-representations that belong to the primary processes;

Fifth stage. Somatic disorganisations; outbursts of various atypical illnesses in relation to the same illnesses of the regressive type; as a result of the disorganisation, illnesses with habitual attacks can herald the first symptom of a progressive disorganisation;

Sixth stage. Emergence of a severe progressive illness, of which the latency period has to be estimated.

The economic viewpoint of Freud's and Marty's models takes into consideration the destiny of excitations in the genesis of reversible illnesses and severe illnesses by foregrounding the failures in their elaboration by the psychic apparatus.

The hidden face of Dora: revisiting Freud's patient (1905)

The conversion hysteria model is very often the only one familiar to young doctors and young psychoanalysts, which leads to rapid and erroneous diagnoses; it is therefore necessary to return to the case of Dora, who presented somatic symptoms in addition to hysterical manifestations. Dora's analysis was addressed by Pierre Marty, Michel Fain, Christian David and Michel de M'Uzan at the 18th Congress of Romance-Language Psychoanalysts in 1967. These members of the Paris School of Psychosomatics rightly paid special attention to Dora's symptoms, recognising that although some of her disorders were conversional in nature, there were others that corresponded to a different pathogenesis. Dora thus presented both hysterical and somatic symptoms (Stora, 1996, p. 232).

Aged 18 years old, despite her opposition, Dora is referred by her father to the family doctor after a fainting episode followed by convulsions and a delirious state. On examination, the clinical picture is striking: many functions seem to be affected–the genito-urinary region by enuresis, dysmenorrhoea, leukorrhoea and possibly ovaritis; the respiratory system by asthma from the age of eight years old, coughing and aphonia; the digestive system by anorexic tendencies, gastralgia, constipation, appendicitis and perityphlitis; and the nervous system, with migraines, asthenia, depressive tendencies, characterological disorders and facial neuralgia. The family antecedents reveal that the father has suffered from a series of illnesses, having had pulmonary tuberculosis for many years; as well as this tuberculosis, there are manifestations of cerebral syphilis, including mental disorders and a detached retina. The father's brother is described as a hypochondriac and his elder sister died following "a marasmus which made rapid advances and the symptoms of which were, as a matter of fact, never fully cleared up" (Freud, 1905, p. 19).

I have chosen to reproduce this clinical picture in order to establish, following the members of the Paris School, the complexity of this multiple symptomatology. In fact, although some disorders unquestionably relate to the mechanism of conversion hysteria, others relate to a different pathogenesis. Freud himself had already made the distinction between somatic disorders of hysterical conversion, which are linked with repressed memories and somatic disorders that present flaws in mental representations (treatment of actual neuroses).[15] From the above-mentioned clinical picture, only respiratory disorders and migraine are symptoms that are not easily associated with conversion hysteria. With regard to this, Freud refers to primary organic disorders that are subsequently used to hysterical ends. He recognises that in his preoccupation with guessing the meaning of dreams, symptoms and associations, he has run the risk of neglecting "another part of the same material" (1905, p. 118). It is my view that, having reached the crossroads of "psychoanalysis" and psychosomatics, Freud chose to develop psychoanalysis as a priority but, as he states, "Psycho-analysts never forget that the mental is based on the organic" (1910, p. 217). Because it involves the body, the conversional symptom opens up another outcome for the psychic conflict, thus indicating the limit of the psychic elaboration. The concept of somatic compliance emphasises the somatic rootedness of sexuality by inscribing it in the framework of the relations between ego instincts and sexual instincts. As David and de M'Uzan state in their presentation to this Congress, the formation of the conversion hysterical symptom requires an organic participation that is first considered in terms of a physiological or pathological process affecting an organ or a function as a result of "constitutional or hereditary factors and the physiological and economic status of a function at the time of a psychic trauma; in other words, this privileged mode of satisfaction with which the subject is connected" (Marty et al., 1968).

Furthermore, the meaning attributed to the symptom is secondarily conferred, provided that there is an adequate capacity for symbolic representation of a desire or conflict and for putting it into a narrative form that relates to the individual's past.

If we are confronted with a problematic of symbolisation capacity, this means—as psychosomatic clinical practice demonstrates—that we are dealing with non-conversional symptomatology. The relation between this kind of pathological functional organisation and this type of conflictual configuration, of which it would be the expression, is non-existent. Consequently, in the context of somatic compliance, there are somatic symptoms that cannot be integrated at the mental level; this means that on the economic level the hysterical mechanism does not provide an adequate outlet for the energies involved and that certain somatic disorders affecting an organ or a function form the object of pure discharge, devoid of meaning, but possibly later resumed, through the psychotherapeutic process, in the form of unconscious fantasy. By providing sustenance to the demand for representations emanating from the unconscious, the therapist facilitates, even induces, in isolated or displaced affects a capacity to be represented, a figurability, without which the neurotic components would not have come so quickly to light. The hypothesis concerning the non-represented, non-signified part, in the Dora case relates to early childhood, something in the drive potential that could not be connected and organised. Psychosomaticians suggest a dual hypothesis to explain the Dora case: an ellipse with two focal points–the hysterical core described by Freud and a psychosomatic core.

This core raises the problem of non-hysterical identifications. This concerns the allergic object relationship as described by Marty; this mode of identification is connected with a need to approach the object as closely as possible to the point of merging with it. The identificatory impulse is more important than the object of identification (sensory, motor or fantasmatic) because this always concerns an idealised mother. *Dora in fact has some symptoms that cannot be linked with the hysterical identification: Leukorrhoea, dyspnoea and migraines.* If this is a plausible hypothesis, somatisation should be considered as a form of "acting in" that implies the preliminary existence of an abnormality in the representation of bodily boundaries.

To explain this in economic terms: in Dora's case history, we are dealing with two paths of energy flow and thus, metaphorically, two basins of attraction for the energy. There is the basin of attraction for the hysterical functioning and a smaller but silently present basin, namely the basin of the allergic functioning. In *L'Ordre psychosomatique* [The psychosomatic order] (1980, pp. 148–149), Marty describes the allergic type of functioning. He states that this involves "an allergic parallel line gradually joining the common central fasciculus"; it "manifests itself relatively independently in its characterological and somatic expressions". I think that we have a manifestation of this allergic parallel line in the abrupt ending to Dora's treatment after three months of psychoanalysis.

To gain a better understanding of the libidinal and somatic fluctuations of this case, I shall begin by using the metaphor suggested by David Ruelle: "Think of water running through a tap. The power applied to the fluid ... is regulated by opening the tap more or less.

If you open the tap a very small amount, you can arrange a *steady* stream of water between the tap and the sink: the column of water appears motionless ... opening the tap a bit more you can (sometimes) arrange regular pulsations of the fluid column; the motion is said to be *periodic* rather than steady. If the tap is opened more, the pulsations become irregular. Finally, if the tap is wide open you see a very irregular flow; you have *turbulence* ... Many objects around us start oscillating or vibrating when we hit them: a pendulum, a metal rod, a string of a musical instrument are readily set into periodic motion. Such a periodic motion is a *mode*. There are also modes of vibration of the column of air in an organ pipe, modes of oscillation of a suspended bridge and so on" (1991, pp. 53–4).

For the libidinal energy that resembles an object through its subjective quality, I shall thus describe the oscillatory libidinal impulses that are induced by topographical dynamic functioning: on the one hand, the drive force arising from the unconscious provokes an upsurge; on the other hand, the ego forces accept it totally or partly by responding to it with a counter-surge: between the two agencies there emerge oscillations with which psychoanalysts are familiar from clinical experience.

In the Dora case, the first basin of attraction belongs to the stable functioning of the psychic oscillator, the repetitive trajectories of which we can trace from the age of six to the age of 18 years. Freud also wonders "whether the symptoms of hysteria ... are necessarily *all* of them psychically determined", concluding that "every hysterical symptom involves the participation of *both* sides. It cannot occur without the presence of a certain degree of *somatic compliance* offered by some normal or pathological process in or connected with one of the bodily organs. And it cannot occur more than once—and *the capacity for repeating itself is one of the characteristics of a hysterical symptom*" (p. 40; my italics).

We are confronted with the manifestation of the periodicity of energy oscillations from the unconscious, simultaneously inducing a repetition compulsion (Jones, 1953).[16] At the time of the consultation (with Freud), Dora's object relations are sufficiently disturbed to be considered as imbued with a repetition compulsion; there is the coughing, associated with migraines, from the age of 12 years, symptoms that coincide with Dora's father's confusional attack; similarly, the aphonia accompanying the cough that enables her to approach and to imitate Mrs K., Dora's father's mistress, thus clearly signifying her desire for him and so on.

However, our explanation goes beyond the repetitive mode of the trajectories of psychic energy in the basin of attraction caused by Dora's psychic trauma. The energy analysis has to be considered in relation to other viewpoints. It seems that some if not all the somatic symptoms relate to a non-conversional somatic reality that is connected, as psychosomaticians have suggested, with the allergic object relationship. Dora grew up in an environment in which her father's life was threatened by a severe illness; this point should be emphasised in order to understand the threat of object loss of the father in Dora's somatic and psychic functioning. From the age of eight years, she suffered from respiratory problems and we might wonder about the possible double meaning of this symptom: reference to the primal scene and/or abnormality of a function that will be used secondarily. With regard to this, Marty (1976, p. 143) refers to the concept of "psychosomatic deferred action" when noting the individual life and death impulses as he wonders about the fact that in certain cases asthma can emerge at the latency period, which does not mean the absence of an asthmatic determinant–that is, a fixation before eight months. *Similarly, the coughing that has to be considered as conversional (sexual connection with the father) does not seem to have absorbed all the available energy; a part of this energy has managed to overload another somatic system with a view to obtaining a discharge devoid of meaning.*

Is Dora suffering from headaches or actual migraines? The diagnosis of actual migraines indicates an allergic type of phenomenon and this symptom appeared at the time of the father's confusional mental attack (fear of losing her father). The study of the allergic object relationship developed by Marty emphasises the following points: essential allergic patients present character traits that reflect a certain way of living; they set about attending to cherished people who are nevertheless interchangeable, either on request or through their own preference: feeding and staying with each other, visiting and exchanging presents. There is a lack of distinction between self and others, constituting a surprising faculty for empathy, as well as a great facility for forming relationships in general and, above all, a surprising aptitude for replacing one object-cathexis with another. Marty points out that for these patients: "The psychotherapist

quickly subdues his illusions concerning the outcome of the interpretations that he gives ... and, however impressed they are by the
analyst's interpretations, the subjects do not elaborate these to the
extent of assimilating them" (1976, p. 154). While admiring Freud's
remarkable interpretive capacities, psychosomaticians think that
there were some deficiencies in Dora's dreaming function, as with
many somatic patients and that as a result *"the features of the psychosomatic core would have become more apparent from an economic perspective than from a dynamic interpretation"*. Not managing to make herself understood at this level, Dora breaks off her treatment, "but was
this recourse exclusively hysterical in nature and would the force of
interpretation alone have been an adequate and sufficient resource
to prevent it? This is questionable" (Marty et al., 1968, p. 700).

In my view one of the effects of the therapeutic process is to reg-
ularise the scope and speed of the psychic oscillator; this leads to
introducing some decelerative and absorptive factors into the
process of regulating emotions connected with life events. Although
it was brief, Freud's psychotherapy was effective in this respect,
since we ascertain a resumption of the oedipal organisation and an
almost total departure from the hysterical basin of attraction. As we
later discover, Dora turns her back on the K family by revealing the
true nature of the relations between her father and Mrs K, as well as
Mr K's seduction attempts directed at her. She partly puts an end to
a traumatic past and marries. In energy terms, I regard this as a
resumption of the economic trajectory and a probable change in the
dynamic state, modifying the trajectories of the general system of
functioning.

In the Dora case, we are dealing as in many somatic problems
with at least two basins of energy attraction, with phenomena occurring at the frontiers of these two basins. This problem relates to the
study of frontiers between basins of attractors; it does not concern
the final stable state of a system but the way in which this system
evolves between several concurrent options. We are confronted with
such options in the interrelation of the psychosomatic basins of
attraction (two sides–one psychic, the other somatic)–which leads us
to envisage several possible steady states for Dora.

The psychic apparatus is thought to regulate the "psychosomatic" whole, supposedly composed of a series of self-regulating
oscillators; when the psychic oscillator is disturbed, fluctuations of

libidinal energy revert to the somatic as a result of the decathexis that affects the somatic sphere; it is thus that respiratory, hormonal and other fluxes begin to be destabilised. To conclude these reflections based on hydrodynamic processes and metaphors, I shall quote Freud who refers to these in writing about the Dora case: "In neurotics their sexual constitution, under which the effects of heredity are included, operates in combination with any accidental influences in their life which may disturb the development of normal sexuality. A stream of water which meets with an obstacle in the river-bed is dammed up and flows back into old channels which had formerly seemed fated to run dry. The motive forces leading to the formation of hysterical symptoms draw their strength not only from repressed *normal* sexuality but also from unconscious perverse activities" (1905, pp. 50–51).

It has been necessary to return to the Dora case because practitioners and doctors continue to refer to hysterical symptoms in order to explain certain somatisations and my purpose in so doing has been to dispel a great many misunderstandings. I shall now present the account of the case of "Latifa" in order to elucidate further the perspective that accompanies the observation of somatic patients.

One of the interns from the department had asked me to help her persuade a patient to take some morphine to relieve her pain; she had also explained to me that she had difficulty communicating with this patient. Concerned to assist her in her therapeutic work and to help this patient, I agreed to talk to Latifa.

Latifa was about 50 years old; she had left the Maghreb a long time since. When I went into her room, I was surprised to see that her window was open, which is unusual since the nurses generally ensure that they are closed for safety reasons. She was lying motionless at the foot of her bed and seemed to be in pain. She looked at me and I had a vague feeling that this investigation would not proceed in the ordinary way. The chair and armchair were covered in various items and the room suddenly seemed to have shrunk. I found these sensory impressions difficult to understand. Were they countertransferential in nature? As when faced with a small child in pain who communicates this to us at an infra-verbal level? Or did this room remind me of a painful situation that had been experienced by someone close to me? I made a mental note of these fleeting impressions. I also realised that I would have to remain standing throughout the conversation, which was uncomfortable. There did not seem to be any space for a psychotherapist!

Latifa stared at me with her black eyes and seemed to be wondering who I might be. I told her that I had come to see her in order to understand her situation and to talk with her, in order to help her in terms of the care being given her. I told her that if she liked she could talk to me about herself and her illness, what she was feeling and thinking ... that I was there to understand and support her. She was the only patient not to call me doctor, as if she had felt that it was different on this occasion. I thought at first that she had not understood what I had told her and then suddenly she talked to me. She moaned that she believed she was going to die and wished to make her peace with God. I found this first statement deeply moving and it reminded me of a similar situation I had experienced three years earlier in which someone very close to me, lying on a stretcher, had put the same question to me (this explains my first sensory perceptions–they brought a painful recent past back to my mind).

It is difficult to remain silent in the face of mortal fear; therefore, using all my powers of persuasion, I tried to reassure her (perhaps reassuring myself as well) and told her that she still had a long time left to live, a very long time (these are ritual phrases used in the Maghreb to bring calm). Of course, I sensed her confusion and distress, diffuse anxieties and a reduction of vital tonus that I attributed to a depressive phase. She looked at me in surprise and seemed to be comforted; she then thanked me in Arabic. The exchange had taken place so quickly that in my formulation I had unconsciously used some turns of phrase based on the Arabic language (naturally because of the emotional force contained in the words). She looked at me more intensely and suddenly said to me: "Are you Jewish?"–"Yes, from the Maghreb". I then sensed a change; I knew that she trusted me. She was talking to someone from her own world. She began by talking about the medicine; she did not want to take morphine, she was afraid of becoming a drug addict and she complained about the doctors who did not provide her with her usual medicines. Then she continued her account in a very factual tone, which again made me pay greater attention, because this colourless intonation revealed to me an automated, almost morbid mental functioning.

"I tried to contact my family in the Maghreb; it is 36 years since I left them (she had never renewed contact with them–this also connoted a traumatic loss of cultural environment–Nathan, 1994). I discovered that my father had died (no affect in her voice) and that my sister was still living in the same town, but I could not reach her on the phone. My children–I have five–don't help me, they don't answer the phone, they leave me alone (again no emotion). I have been here since last Monday but I have not yet been able to inform my younger son (after a slight hesitation) ... he will come".

"You have certainly had a difficult life ..."

This simple and commonplace utterance opened the way: "You know, my husband beat me, he burnt my arms with acid (she showed me the burn marks); but my father also beat me" ... (always this actual trauma relating back to the trauma of the past).

Latifa had divorced fourteen years earlier; at first, her husband had taken her children away from her; she then succumbed to depression. Two years later, she began to suffer from sight disorders (episodes of visual blurring and headaches); the following year, she underwent a total hysterectomy. She was hospitalised for multiple sclerosis and I asked her if she understood why she had all her illnesses and what her thoughts were about this (This slightly strange formulation was intended to stimulate an inner enquiry into the relationship between the patient and her illnesses, the role played by these and particularly through the introspection for her to resume a degree of mental functioning).

We had moved seamlessly from her children to "her" illnesses–"Oh, you know, this illness began fifteen years ago, but I have had lots of other illnesses; a hiatus hernia when I was 23 years old, then appendicitis, a pulmonary embolism, a gastrectomy, two episodes of cerebral phlebitis nine years ago and asthma for about 20 years".

This is a polysomatising patient–or multi-medicalised, as my medical colleagues say. The multiple sclerosis had begun two years before her divorce; I listened to her carefully, but at a deeper level I was asking myself many questions about the solidity of her psychic functioning and the highly specific way in which she was very quickly overwhelmed by the events in her family life.

She went on to talk about her professional life: "I started working in fashion and then, as I was not making a living, I sold fruit and vegetables at the market; it was hard ... as well as bringing up five children". In this brief silence, I pictured years of suffering and deprivation.

"And your daughters aren't helping you?"–"They don't want me to phone them. I am afraid of going back home; I would like to return to my home country to die ..."

The conversation seemed to end as it had begun. With her gaze that expressed acute distress, bed-bound without any family visits or hope of a possible life in the near future, in a sense she was in a dead-end situation. This is, I think, what she wanted to tell me by talking about death (there was no life-threatening prognosis). I know from experience that it is possible to revive patients and I addressed her in a mixture of Arabic and French and by calling her "Sister" ("Ma soeur"), as I had learnt to do as a child, rather than "Madame". "You are going to live and my colleagues are going to help you with all the powers at their disposal; I know that you are a bit isolated here; do you want me to ask someone from the Muslim community (the Mosque, perhaps) to come and see you to keep you company?" I realise that this procedure is not very analytic, but what else could be done in this kind of desperate situation?!

She looked at me and I felt that she was directing her thoughts towards me in order to thank me: she uttered the ritual words of blessing. Then I left her and went to find my young colleague. We both returned to Latifa's room and, after some persuasion, she agreed to take the medicine.

The nurses and auxiliaries complained about her; in fact, unconsciously, Latifa was doing everything she could to make the care staff loathe her; they wanted to hit her, just as her father and husband had done–evidence that the repetition compulsion was at work. Latifa was rejected by the doctors, the care staff, her husband and her children ... (a classic case of "A child is being beaten"–Freud, 1919).

She asked me to leave the door open as I left; she wanted to be able to see the hustle and bustle in the corridor. I took this as a positive sign of resuming interest in life. As I left her, I made phone contact with a member of the Muslim community, as I had promised her.

Commentary

According to the psychosomatic investigative method that I am proposing, I shall first establish a chronological connection between life events and the emergence of illnesses (according to the available information). The two series of events may have interrelated progression with the same probable meaning, without this necessarily making them specifically causal; furthermore, we do not know anything about the hereditary genetic variables and we have little information about the early years of her life. I shall also be putting forward some fuller observations in the chapters that follow. It goes without saying that such observations draw on clinical and theoretical experience. Latifa was 16 years old when she left Algeria with her husband; she had had five children over about ten years and had begun to suffer from somatic disorders from the age of 23 years old with the hiatus hernia. Nine years later, she underwent a gastrectomy, following a vagotomy and a pulmonary embolism. All the disorders seem to have appeared during the same period (when the patient was 31–32 years old), along with respiratory disorders (asthma) and digestive disorders. Seven years later, she divorced and a period of depression ensued; she was temporarily separated from her children and two years after her divorce she was suffering from sight disorders and underwent a hysterectomy, followed by headaches and two episodes of cerebral phlebitis and finally a severe attack of multiple sclerosis twelve years after her divorce. It is certainly possible that the initial sight disorders were early signs of the multiple sclerosis, but this cannot be certain, since this is a symptom common to many illnesses. The clinical profile is yet more complex, but for the purposes of this discussion I shall emphasise *the latency periods between life events and the emergence of somatic disorders*.

The first event is her departure from Algeria, the emigration of this family. Latifa was still very young, an adolescent who was still undergoing the psychosexual maturation process; I had some doubts as to whether the genital oedipal organisation was established. This last stage of development had probably never taken place; she had remained fixed at a pregenital stage of development. Significantly, sadomasochistic relations–with the father, husband,

medical and hospital staff etc.–could be observed, as well as character traits and a point of psychic fixation, giving rise to repetitive
behaviour.

The succession of illnesses appeared following the difficulties
encountered: divorce and temporary abduction of the children.
Somatic deterioration is a slow process; the disorders do not appear
suddenly. The conflicts with her husband take place over the course
of five pregnancies and in the years that follow.

The emotional overload induced by the conflictual relations with
her husband fuels the masochistic drive excitations (internal excitations in the psychic apparatus), but this apparatus is flooded in what
is likely to be a phase of essential depression. It is neutralised and
here we witness a first modification of the patient's libidinal economy; the libido returns to the ego at the level of oral fixation and not
at the level of the apparent anal fixation. The flooding of the psychic
apparatus means that the excitations could not be connected by the
mechanism of the secondary process. However, the problem of a
minimal functioning of the psychic apparatus is posed.

*This reduction is the consequence of the transmission of the overload of
excitations of the psychic system (primary narcissism) to the somatic markers and to the coenaesthetic organisation, which consequently instigates the
beginning of the disturbance in the sub-systems of biological homeostasis.*

The neurosciences demonstrate that the neuronal circuits that are
most important for survival exist in the brain stem and the hypothalamus. The hypothalamus is the site of regulation of the endocrine,
pituitary, thyroid, adrenal and sexual glands–and the functioning of
the immune system. In coordination with the structures of the limbic
system and the brain stem, the hypothalamus ensures the regulation
of the internal environment, which corresponds to the sum of biochemical processes that occur in an organism. "Life depends on those
biochemical processes" being kept within a suitable range, since
excessive departures from that range, at key points in the composite
profile, *may result in disease or death*" (Damasio, 1995, pp. 118–119). As
concerns the patient under observation, the first biological functions
to succumb according to the above-described processes are the respiratory and alimentary functions. There are stages in this somatisation
process, since there has been a transition from a hiatus hernia to a gastrectomy through an intermediate range of gastric disorders. Latifa's
divorce followed by a depression may constitute a traumatic event of

the kind commonly described by psychosomaticians in their anamneses. We know that an event of this importance does not happen from one day to the next. This event is both preceded and followed by years of confrontation. Once again, I emphasise the concept of "constant stress" to explain one of the possible factors in somatisations; the psychic apparatus, the principal role of which is to elaborate the "quantum" of internal and external excitations generated by events, fulfils the primary role in preventing somatic illnesses, in addition to biological processes.

The severe somatic disorders do not appear until fifteen years after her marriage. Latifa told me clearly that the husband took over from the father's sadistic behaviour: "I was beaten by my husband". This expression corresponds to the second phase described by Freud in "A child is being beaten" (1919), the incestuous love fantasy, transformed from the genital meaning, "my father loves me", under the influence of regression to the anal-sadistic pregenital organisation into "I am being beaten by my father"; the fantasy has become masochistic. This mode of functioning emphasises the weakness of the genital organisation, as I had suggested in my investigation; similarly, I had emphasised the masochistic factor as the predominant character trait. Repression is the mechanism at work: "Thus repression is operative here in three ways: it renders the consequences of the genital organization unconscious, it compels that organization itself to regress to the earlier sadistic-anal stage and it transforms the sadism of this stage into masochism, which is passive and again in a certain sense narcissistic" (1919, p. 194). As long as excitations can be managed in this mode, masochism is the guardian of life, as Rosenberg wrote: "It is this that teaches us that certain increases in excitational tension, which are actually of the order of pain or displeasure, can be experienced as a pleasure" (1991, p. 60). Masochism has become fatal for Latifa; with fatal masochism, the subject cathects the excitation to find pleasure in it, thus making the discharge in the object satisfaction superfluous. We are thus dealing with a transformation of the libidinal cathexis, which indicates to us a blockage of the life drive that is normally centred on the object relationship such that fatal masochism "can lead the subject towards death by siderating the normal functioning of the libido and self-preservation" (Rosenberg, 1991, p. 85). *The sideration of the psychic apparatus by fatal masochism is one of the modes of instigation of somatisations.*

It becomes easier to understand the threat hanging over Latifa if we consider the divorce as a traumatic event that brings the rupture of the masochistic homeostasis obtained in the relationship with her husband. At this period, has she been through an essential type of depression (Marty, 1968, p. 595)? I have no proof of this, but it seems likely to be the case. It seems that failures in the psyche undergoing a phase of sideration have given way—according to my theoretical approach—to somatic regulation by the somatic agencies of bioregulation.

Here I am putting forward the hypothesis of an equilibrium that alternates between the functioning of the psychic system and the somatic system throughout human lives. The former secures the coordination and cohesion of the whole; the latter takes over when the former fails.

The first failure, and thus in neuronal terms the *first changes in the initial conditions*, took place fifteen years after the departure from Algeria: Latifa had had five children and her relations with her husband were deteriorating, but she was not yet contemplating divorce. In North Africa, it is generally the men who instigate divorce or repudiation proceedings. It requires considerable moral strength for a woman to be able to resolve to separate from her husband. Unable to confront her husband and in an extremely weak condition, Latifa battled for her survival; here it is the self-preservative drives that are in the foreground, indicating even at this stage a deep regression since the masochism, as guardian of life, could no longer operate. Over two years, the siderated psychic system gave way to somatic regulation; the body took over but the overload of excitations threatened the homeostatic equilibrium of two functions: pulmonary embolism and gastrectomy.

The brain functions on the basis of the survival principle; it is equipped with an information system that indicates to it at every moment the specific image of the body (conveyed by the sensation of living) and the state of biological regulation. The patient's respiratory (asthma attacks) and alimentary functions were disturbed by the first modifications of the initial state; there was a life-threatening prognosis at the time of the pulmonary embolism. Through the organisation of the body into biological subsystems, the organism's survival was secured; shortly after the surgical operations, there was a resumption of psychic activity for more than four years, then a further traumatic crisis caused by the divorce, followed by an essential depression.

For Marty in certain subjects the constant or repeated excesses and, finally, the accumulation of excitations at the psycho-affective level, without any possibilities of mental elaboration and the resumption of an essential depression (often resumption of a childhood depression or a more pronounced resumption of a latent depression) induce a process of progressive disorganisation and the onset of severe illnesses.

This means that Latifa's first somatic afflictions, due to the first failure of psychic functioning–sideration–weakened the psyche, which was flooded at the time of the second traumatic shock (the divorce). On several occasions, I have referred to the phase of essential depression, a phase during which the diversity and richness of psychic functioning seem to disappear, a phase accompanied by a sensation of coldness emanating from the subject in pain and by an absence of emotional manifestation. Neuroscientific research seems to concur here with the propositions of hypotheses put forward by psychosomaticians who are psychoanalysts concerning depressive states and the emotional expression that accompanies them: "Along with negative body states, the generation of images is slow, their diversity small and reasoning inefficient ... When negative body states recur frequently, or when there is a sustained negative body state, as happens in a depression, the proportion of thoughts which are likely to be associated with negative situations does increase and the style and efficiency of reasoning suffer" (1995, p. 147). Damasio describes as a state or a series of states in the neuronal system that which psychosomaticians have attributed to deficiencies of the psychic apparatus.

In terms of oscillations in somatic energy, our patient's equilibrium, disturbed by the various traumas of her life, moves from a steady equilibrium to a series of unstable states through a progressive increase in the parameters of energic overload, unbalancing the threshold values that ensure somatic functioning (Bergé et al., 1997).

To conclude, in Chapters One and Two I have put forward the concepts and notions that I intend to use to illustrate the clinical observations in the chapters that follow. Having reintroduced the psychic apparatus into the totality of the functioning of living organisms, I postulated the principle that there are intermediate centres existing between this and the totality of somatic functions with reference to Damasio's findings and Spitz's works. The somatic markers and the coenaesthetic organisation, the first somatopsychic organisation, seem to me to secure the transition between all the levels of the living being. I have also resituated psychic functioning in its surrounding context, which deeply influences psychic structuring, which has evolved profoundly over the 20th century. These mental structures (Stora, 1994; Appendix 1) are well defined by Marty's notion of "mentalisation" and they enable us better to determine the progress of somatic patients. Finally, following many psychosomaticians, I adopt the hypothesis that the economic point of view is predominant in assessing the psychic functioning of these patients. In this respect, I am extending the research studies by emphasising the loss of psychosexual qualities from the libidinal energy returning to the body at the time of traumas and constant stress. Converting back into somatic energy, it follows the laws of fluctuations defined by physico-chemical factors; I suggest that we can observe, metaphorically, these kinds of energy fluctuations and oscillations in the psychic sphere.

CHAPTER THREE

Amanda, Arnaud, Alice, Sandrine and Emma–somatisations and regressions

"Somatic diseases generally stem from the individual's inadequacies with regard to the living conditions that he encounters".

Pierre Marty (1990, p. 48)

When we examine somatic patients in a hospital setting at the request of doctors in the department, the conditions are different from those found in psychosomatic psychoanalytic institutions. The psychologist or psychoanalyst who is also a psychosomatician is in a difficult position because he is not conducting a psychiatric examination (with which somatician doctors are familiar) and he has to communicate the essential findings of his examination to doctors in a matter of minutes so as to assist in the patient's care in a way that complements the medicine being given. Beyond the difference in scientific approach, there is also the question of the terms in which the diagnosis is formulated: how are we to communicate the provisional findings of an examination to a doctor who has no knowledge of the psychosomatic and psychoanalytic models that form the point of reference? We can thus recognise the scale of difficulty surrounding the exchange and interaction between the various parties who are addressing problems of illness and health.

The interviews that I am going to set out took place at the bedside of patients at the request of various staff with whom I have worked. This has been a fascinating clinical experience and with each patient I have met I have tried to find the most appropriate solutions in order to recommend a suitable form of psychotherapeutic follow-up care. Needless to say, many patients are deeply hostile to any exploration of the psychological dimension of their illnesses, insisting that it is their body that is ill, not their "mind", which relates back to mediaeval fears of madness. Also, doctors who are subject to relentless time pressures tend to adopt two main types of behaviour. On the one hand, they may think illness has a "medical" cause (lesional, mechanically based, viral etc.) and not want the psychosomatician to intervene since, according to the current emphasis in medical science on the body-psyche dichotomy, such an examination would be superfluous. Alternatively, the psychosomatician does intervene, having obtained the patient's consent, in order to explore the psychological dimension. In this case, the doctor often refers to the classical model of conversion hysteria in order to understand symptoms that are not strictly somatic in origin and expects the psychosomatician to confirm his intuition. Unlike somaticians who strongly emphasise the bio-medical model of disease, other doctors who are more sensitive to the relational dimension with patients encourage psychosomaticians to play a more active role in seeking a multi-disciplinary understanding of the symptoms; from this viewpoint, it is important to develop knowledge and skill concerning the psychosomatic model from the perspective that I am presenting in this work, namely a multi-dimensional and multi-causal approach.

In this chapter, I shall present some clinical examinations with a view to illustrating the concepts put forward in the preceding chapters. As indicated above, in the examination I give consideration to the psychosomatic equilibrium, having evaluated the various modes of excitational discharge, namely the work of mental elaboration (thought), behaviours, emotional life and somatic history (illnesses). In common with all psychosomaticians, I am thereby emphasising the economic point of view ("mental energy") while making recourse to regular or irregular oscillatory equilibria of this "energy", which is set in motion by the contingencies of daily life in all its dimensions: family, professional and so on. Foregrounding the economic point of view, the psychosomatic approach accounts for the connections between every level of the living organism and thus provides an understanding of anomalies in psychic and somatic functioning.

A high quantum of excitations leads the psychic apparatus to undertake the work of elaboration by means of the preconscious (evaluation of its density). Here we are confronted with two possible pathways for somatisations: 1. with an average level of excitations and where mentalisation meets all the criteria, clinical practice shows that we can anticipate the onset of somatic complaints that are usually spontaneously reversible; 2. with a high level of excitations and where mentalisation does not meet all the criteria, there is a strong probability that we will witness the onset of severe progressive complaints.

In this chapter, I shall address the problematic of somatisations that emerge following psychic regressions and, in the next chapter, somatisations that emerge following progressive disorganisations. I shall use the concepts set out in the preceding chapters relating to the transmission of excitations that occurs through the instigation of the homeostatic oscillators in the various bodily organs and functions following failures of the psychic apparatus. Consideration must also be given to the pressures emanating from the social, economic and cultural environment that threaten psychosomatic functioning. It is important to understand the alternating phases; that is, between psychic malfunctioning and somatic turbulence.

Amanda–disorders in physical activity

It is preferable not to consult the medical file before the examination in order to be able to compare the first diagnosis *ex post facto* with information obtained from the file and, more importantly, to evaluate the patient's own perception and experience of the illness, as well as ways in which he may be emphasising certain information about its progress or consciously or unconsciously concealing particular symptoms or information. In fact, it takes much longer to establish a psychosomatic diagnosis than a standard medical diagnosis; the first statement is often provisional and it may continue to develop throughout the week or even longer. This difference in time and pace needs to be indicated, as it gives rise to communication problems between doctors and psychosomaticians (psychoanalysts and psychologists).

When I entered the room in one of the wings of the department, Amanda lay semi-reclined in her bed, smiling, relaxed and looking rather pleased to be in hospital for a course of treatment; she seemed happy to accept the presence of a "psychologist" and was very willing to talk to me.

"I was a professional; I worked for a big company. I'm here today because I have a recurrence of discal hernia and I need a second operation. Three years ago, I woke up and found my lower limbs were paralysed. I responded very well and I fought really hard. It was a one-in-thousand probability, but three months later I had recovered; I walked on crutches for a while and could almost manage without them by the end of a year. Today I have lumbago pains in my buttocks and legs, pain across an extensive area and contractions–my sufferings date back to the beginning of August that year".

Amanda was 37 years old. As I sat at her bedside, she told me about her sufferings, her operation, her hardships and her pain, but she did not communicate her emotion to me; I felt nothing in this exchange, which was a statement of facts. I wondered, however, if she were not trying to protect herself from remembering the events by distancing herself from the emotions that had accompanied them. She moved in her bed from time to time by leaning on her pillow or alternately tucking one leg under another, pressing down on her right leg or her left leg; she was wearing trousers and a jumper and had remained fully clothed in her bed. She had just arrived and it seemed that I had interviewed her before she had seen a doctor and the nurses had had time to attend to her. We were in an intermediate time and space that was conducive to exchange.

"I was given some scanner-guided injections; there was some improvement in April and May last year, but towards the end of June and beginning of July I really wondered how I was going to live with my suffering; I left the hospital in tears. I was going to have to learn to live with it".

"Live with my suffering" is an expression that is occasionally used by patients either because they are despairing of medicine and are becoming aware of the limitations of treatments or because a masochistic type of psychic dimension is at work for reasons that are highly specific to elucidate, or because physical pain is substituting for mental pain, playing a role in the psycho-affective equilibrium.

"Do you think that your sufferings now might be connected with any bad experience you might have had in your personal life?"

"One of my sons, who is fourteen years old, recently left me to go and live with his father, although I brought this child up all alone after my divorce; I left his father when I was pregnant with him and now he has gone. His brother, who is two years older, left me three years ago ... I remarried when I was in a physiotherapy nursing home, paralysed. I got divorced twelve years ago, but today my ex-husband is still attacking and harassing me. I was the one who left; he was hitting me. I tried to commit suicide twice–three years after my divorce and again one year ago. I had thought it all through; I knew I was about to lose my second son to my husband ... professionally, I am at a complete standstill".

Amanda had briefly described to me the traumatic events in her life over the past fourteen years. It requires great resilience to confront this kind of onslaught. I continued our interview with a view to discovering what repercussions these traumas might be having now on her psychic and somatic functioning: was her sleep disturbed? Sleep! "I don't sleep at night; I get to sleep in the early hours of the morning. All day long I am bored, I knit, I read novels ... you know, I am a woman of action, I know I am not as strong as I was, I was working in a big company, I had a responsible position. I was given some financial training at my workplace and I supplemented it with a university diploma by taking exams until I was 30 years old. I really enjoy learning; I am hungry for knowledge".

She has a strong intellectual curiosity, which extends to knowledge of her medical file–fibrosis and so on–all the medical vocabulary of her illness. Many patients have a thorough knowledge of their medical files, as if to overcome the illness and symptoms in a magical mode.

We then moved on to her family relationships and her parents: "My father died, almost nine years ago, of liver cancer; my mother is still alive; she is 66 years old". Amanda was the last-born of her siblings; she has two sisters and a brother. "I had a very bad relationship with my father, who blamed me for being an accident–when I was little, I wished he would go away for ever; I still haven't mourned him. I ran away when I was fifteen; I had gone to the library, the only place my father would allow me to go and I was late getting home–I was frightened ... I ran away".

What might this brief silence after "I was frightened ..." mean? Later in the session, as if in response to the question that I was silently formulating, Amanda told me that she had taken refuge for several days at the house of a woman known to her boyfriend (?) who was already grown-up. Did her father have any inkling of his daughter's secret love relationship (oedipal conflict and object choice in the father's image)?

"My father had beaten me ever since I was a child. I was beaten along with my mother, but the other children weren't–he was violent to my mother–I came back home (after running away) and, although it was difficult, at my mother's insistence I asked him to forgive me". This was how Amanda described to me her return after running away, but it seemed to me that she was referring to other circumstances in a slightly mysterious past that I was beginning to discern.

Amanda described the reconciliation scene with her father on her return; he tried to take her in his arms when she asked his forgiveness, but she was terribly frightened of this physical contact and referred to her father's "ambiguity". Did this apply only to her father? What about her own "ambiguity?"

"After this incident, they wanted to put me in a home. By the time I was eighteen, I was independent. I had already been living in my own flat for two years–with my diploma in my hand, I had gone back to the large company where I still work now. My brother and sisters are in the same field as me; you know, in those days, there was still some work available".

Referring to a scene of her father's violence must have provoked the association with other memories, which attested her capacity to move between past and present, as well as the wealth of associations connected with these events (wealth of the preconscious and symbolisation capacity). Amanda then re-lived another scene of her father's violence.

"When I was being confirmed, when I was eleven or twelve years old, my father started going through all the rooms in the flat one evening in a fit of rage, on the pretext that he had lost a hanger". Amanda was frightened again, but she said no more about it.

(The foundations were laid for sado-masochistic relational potentialities with her future suitors.)

"I have good memories of being with my brother and my sisters. There was a three-year age-gap between my brother and me ... he is the eldest ... when I was little, I preferred playing with toy cars and marbles with my brother; as an adolescent, I only ever went out to go to the library, I never went to a party or anywhere".

I thought about my own associations to the image of a family that seemed to have strongly cathected physical activity and I explored this behavioural aspect of excitational discharge: did every member of the family share in this behaviour?

"We all played sport–I liked classical dance and did this until I was thirteen; then I had to stop because there was no money to pay for the lessons–I still liked it but I had to give it up. I took the entrance competition for the conservatory. I replaced dancing with basketball and then I did artistic gymnastics–I liked physical activity–I always have done–I really liked beating (!) the others; being the best at the sport I chose. I played the piano until I was seventeen–my mother's piano–but running appeals to me more".

Amanda was therefore talking about behaviours deployed since earliest childhood, thus she preferred "running" ... (like her father or her mother, I wondered).

Amanda continued the associative chain to her mother–music–since she had been telling me about the piano: "My present husband is a musician; we got to know each other at the nursing home where he was being treated after a serious car accident–it was a bolt from the blue–it is now three years since we got to know each other and we have got married" (shortly before her son left their home).

My twin sisters are two years older than me–my mother was physically exhausted (overburdened with work). I could read before I went back to school and I skipped the preparatory course–my mother was a paediatric nurse then–since my father died, she has travelled a lot–she took some exams and became a tour guide".

Amanda did not seem to be impressed by her mother's achievements; she showed no admiration for her change of profession and retraining ... "You know–we are all very dynamic. My father repaired machines for a large company and then he left to work for himself. He became a driver; he worked nights and came back early in the morning. I was ashamed of my father–had he always had an odd attitude towards me, or did I imagine that?"

"He often told me, "Shut up, you–you weren't wanted, shut your trap"".

"My mother had broken fingers on several occasions because of my father's violence–their bedroom was next to mine'. She did not continue with this associative chain; the proximity of her parents' bedroom brought back a short dream that she remembered as follows: "I am being attacked and I am paralysed with fear". The rest was lost in silence, which may be connected with the contemplation of a primal scene (proximity of her parents' bedroom) and the oedipal desire experienced in a sado-masochistic mode.

"For several months, I have been thinking about motherhood; we would like to have a child–I miss bringing up a young child. I was 20 years old when I had my eldest son–I haven't seen my children growing up".

She returned to one of the sources of trauma and frustration in her current situation–the loss of her children. Remembering her children brought her past back to the surface again.

"I don't have childhood memories; I only have bad memories–my father's increasing violence over the years".

Amanda then talked about her first husband's violence, saying that he had been gentle at the time of their marriage but all his symptoms had begun when she was pregnant with her second child. He had an obsessive fear of running people over in the street–he would drive back to check that no one had been killed.

Her husband's violence towards Amanda reminded me of her father's violence and, in particular, his wish that Amanda had never seen the light of day–this "fundamental violence" on the part of fathers towards unwanted children. What a strange coincidence to have a husband who became violent along with obsessional symptoms when she was pregnant with her second child! The husband's obsessional symptoms seemed to reveal his unconscious desire to reject the second child–a murderous wish revealed by his fear of running over pedestrians, accompanied by compulsive checking and the manifestation of physical violence for nearly one year towards Amanda.

"The children's custody was settled last year after some abuse and a court case; he is still behaving aggressively towards me, since in March this year I have to go back to court again because he is asking me for alimony!

I am isolated–I only keep in touch with my family and my new parents-in-law (the second husband's parents)–my mother-in-law is helping me, as are my sisters and my sister-in-law–my colleagues have stopped coming to see me; also, I have moved house ... but I am still employed by my company".

This provided some reassurance on the professional level; she would be able to resume her activities. At least there were no threats emanating from this aspect of her environment, which was therefore not a source of excitations.

At the end of the session, she told me about her relations with her husband: "They were satisfactory, but since I have been in pain again, it has become painful (no more sexual relations) and I don't want to do it. My husband is frustrated; he more or less accepts the situation but it is difficult for him".

Once again, this situation was described without emotional affect; then Amanda returned to the present situation, as if we had been through all the problems and our conversation was therefore coming to a close: "I am pleased to have come back to hospital–I was getting impatient for this–I am going to have perfusions for fifteen days. It is only fifteen days since I was about to try and commit suicide because of the pain and the life I am leading. I realise that the problem of the relationship with my father is unresolved".

Commentary

I shall next analyse the transmission of fluctuations in the psychic apparatus, which is temporarily flooded, with a selective impact on the locomotor functions in a subject whose mental qualities are beyond doubt.

As a result of her family environment, from a very early age Amanda has strongly cathected physical activity, which has served as a favoured means of excitational discharge–from playing with her elder brother's toy cars to sport, classical dance, basketball and so on, to which we can add the piano as physical exercise–moving her fingers–rather than sublimatory activity. This artistic activity seems to have acquired an objectal and sublimatory dimension with her remarriage, bringing her closer to her mother, since her second husband was chosen in her mother's image. She is orally fixated since there is dependency on tobacco and alcohol, which she has used for the last ten years (information communicated after our interview) and also anally fixated since physical activity is a sign of muscular and mental control. It is these two aspects that are put forward as solutions to the anxiety arising from confronting internal conflicts. The anamnesis reveals the patient's arrested psychosexual development, since the father's violence first delayed then prevented the establishment of the oedipal organisation; hence, the inhibition of genital energy. During adolescence, she has cathected the aggressive drives and motricity. The maturational process seems to be stuck at the phallic stage, facilitating her autonomy and professional career.

Her father's death, the departure of her two children and her divorce constitute a series of traumatic events that have reactivated the oedipal problematic, thus revealing the incapacity of her mental organisation to elaborate (failure of mentalisations) the surplus of excitations induced by these events. The inhibition of physical activity stems from her father's past violence because suppression of the aggressive drives prevents Amanda from discharging the "quantum of excitations" through muscular pathways; the failures of mentalisation also prevent any mental elaboration of these traumas, at the very least *on an intermittent and temporary basis.*

As it is worked out by the anamnesis, the structure of the psychic apparatus economically favours excitational discharge into muscular activities and oral satisfactions (such as cigarettes). The patient therefore presents zones of adequate mentalisation in some facets of the ego and lacunae in others, which is reminiscent of what Marty terms "neurotics with uncertain mentalisation", who appear hypersymbolic at times and hyposymbolic at others;[17] this uncertainty concerning the stability of psychic functioning makes an argument for caution in formulating the diagnosis.

Under the impact of the various traumatic events, the anomalies in mental functioning progressively lead to violent fluctuations in psychic energy. The inhibition of genital energy produces a regression to points of anal and oral fixation in motricity. However, a large proportion of the anxiety generated by confronting the conflicts then fails to find any outlets (discharge) either through mental elaboration, which is deficient, or through directly muscular discharge. In

Amanda's situation of constant stress, somatic energy instigates the bio-regulation processes that activate hormonal secretions, which act continuously on the musculature. The musculature then contracts to the point of exhaustion, causing mechanical traumas at the weakest points of the skeleton (vertebrae), vulnerable parts of the body, on which strong demands are made by events in Amanda's history. This involves somatic vulnerability and also somatic compliance. Excitational discharge cannot take place outside the body, since the suppression of the aggressive drives continues as a process; as this energy cannot be bound at the preconscious level, it then converts back into somatic energy, generating muscular contractions.

The latency periods between events and somatisations are as follows: N + 3 – three years after her divorce, a suicide attempt and first operation (discal hernia); n + 4 – one year later, her father's death, followed six years later by the departure of one of her children; n + 10 – second operation, then two years later (n + 12) the departure of her second child, leading to hospitalisation and temporary paralysis of her lower limbs. I think that the change of equilibrium in the family environment combined with failures of mental elaboration have gradually amplified the psychic oscillations. When these oscillations became turbulent and prone to flooding, leading to instability, they spread to the apparatus that has been subject to the most demands and psychic cathexis throughout her life. In Amanda's particular case, we can observe: 1. a steady state in the psychic apparatus is disturbed, the initial state is gradually abandoned and the turbulence threshold is reached; 2. a transition to the steady state in the soma, disturbed in its functioning, resisting for many years before attaining a new state of equilibrium without a return to the initial state.

The current hospitalisation temporarily constitutes a protective environment in which her anxieties are diminished and homeostasis is provisionally restored. The hospital is thus acting as a protective barrier, the quintessential primary maternal function.

What will happen to Amanda when she leaves the department? Will her mental organisation resume its earlier functioning? Amanda's psychic functioning is relatively stable and it should be possible for a psychotherapeutic treatment to bring about a substantial reinforcement in her psychic defences in the future. Will Amanda regain the full use of her bodily movements? Only doctors would be able to answer this type of question. It goes without saying that the re-establishment of physical activity through relaxation, physiotherapy treatments and so on will facilitate a narcissistic restitution and the return to a new steady state that is already probable.

Arnaud–managing at risk of his life

Myocardial infarction is a syndrome caused by inadequate arterial blood supply to a part of the myocardium, which carries the risk of myocardial necrosis and death. Although the causes of this interruption to blood flow are impossible to determine in the majority of cases, an event of this kind is certainly linked with a specific process; moreover, it is probable that the central nervous system is itself linked to these processes (Noble, 1989). Since every case of myocardial infarction involves different processes to varying degrees, it follows that there are several different types. I shall not elaborate on the medical research aspect of this disorder, but I shall emphasise some of the aspects considered by researchers in order to explain some of the processes at work; this somatic dimension is necessary for the remainder of my argument.

The pathogenic process associated with myocardial infarction is atherosclerosis. The vast majority of patients who die of myocardial infarction or sudden cardiac death present a severe atherosclerosis of one or several coronary arteries. Most research studies have found that at least 90% of cardiac organs in patients dying of myocardial infarction had a coronary artery that had been reduced by over 75% in diameter by atherosclerosis. While atherosclerosis is clearly implicated in the pathogenesis of myocardial infarction, psychosocial and other factors also play a role in the development of conditions that are conducive to its aetiology. Although the transformative processes that lead to the high cholesterol level in atherosclerosis in the coronary arteries are not fully understood, many research studies suggest that excitation of the central nervous system results in the activation of either the pituitary gland or the adrenomedullary sympathetic system, or both, and thus contributes to an increase in lipid levels, which ultimately results in atherosclerosis. Constant stress was thus the source of the high cholesterol levels found in American accountants in the period preceding the fiscal declaration of 15 April, whereas the same levels were low at other periods of the year. The psychosocial factor is found in many studies, such as the research conducted by Lapin & Cherkovich (1971) into psychosocial stress in baboons, which used various methods to induce behavioural changes that finally induced neuroses and somatic disorders such as hypertension, coronary deficiencies and myocardial infarctions. Research conducted by Shekelle, Ostfeld and Paul into changes in social status over the course of working life, such as differentials between educational level, income level and the post held, or between status in adulthood and class of origin and so on, distinguished five categories of differential or discrepancy that enabled them to ascertain that individuals suffering from cardiac diseases had experienced at least four of these situations of social differential during their lifetime. For these men, the risk of myocardial infarction was 19 times higher than for those who had no differential criteria and three times higher than for those with only a single criterion.

The psychosocial variable that formed the object of the most extensive research studies fell within the category of the behaviours of action-orientated men and women; this led to drawing up profiles termed "Type A" or "Type B". These names were suggested by Dr Friedman (Friedman & Rosenman, 1959; Friedman & Ulmer, 1984). Type A individuals display the following characteristics: strong aggression, ambition, a competitive attitude, impatience and, finally, an acute sense of the urgency of time. Two large-scale studies (Feinleib et al., 1975, 1978) found significant correlations between Type A behaviour and ischaemic heart disorders. In Framingham's study, which was based on a 300-item questionnaire describing Type A, researchers found that Type A men aged between 45 and 64 years of age had double the risk of Type B men (Feinleib et al., 1980) of a myocardial infarction over the next eight years. The incidence of coronary disease was significantly correlated with Type A behaviour, parental history (of heart disease), diabetes, years of school attendance, tobacco addiction, high blood pressure and high levels of cholesterol, triglycerides and betalipoproteins. The research conducted by Friedman & Rosenman (1959) came under some criticism; this related, in fact, to the methodological difficulty of establishing the Type A profile using the standard questionnaire. This requires special training and in the best case the investigator manages to place 70-80% of the people who might fit the profile in this category. At present, Framingham's study uses the method with the highest success rate for assessing Type A behaviour. Many other studies provide a point of comparison with this approach and, although it is clear that Type A behaviour is associated with cardiac ischaemia in certain demographic groups, it is not known for certain which aspects of the behaviour are connected with the heart disorder. With these precautions in mind, we can now move on to the account of Arnaud's case. Arnaud is a company director whom I met while I was conducting a survey into professional stress; it was not possible to conduct a psychoanalytic anamnesis, nor a psychosomatic examination. Arnaud's own testimony is valuable in the light of the research that I have reported above.

Arnaud's battle with the invisible man

Arnaud was the director of a subsidiary of a large international corporation; this 50-year-old man, who was bounding with energy and impatient, seemed to have an inner anxiety that emerged intermittently during the interview. He struck me as both solid and fragile, as if he needed to be helped; when his secretary had shown me into his office, I observed that she threw him a very concerned glance (in a maternal way). Arnaud was someone who spent a lot of time with his colleagues and knew how to manage his schedule; he proudly showed me how well organised his office was. He knew that I was conducting research into professional stress and he appeared to want me to assess him, or was it that I would play an unconscious role that I had yet to explain? He again emphasised time: "All my time-planning for schedules and meetings is based on a period of extensive development and mental preparation". He carefully chose his immediate colleagues, who complemented his own personality. Responding to an inner compulsion, he returned to the subject of time, emphasising its scarcity.

Why did Arnaud have so little time available? What did he want to tell me? Perhaps that he sensed he had very little time left!

In the interview, he then addressed the problem of the insecurity that threatens the president's role; he explained to me that the efficient running of this international corporation required the implementation of a policy to rotate the directors of the subsidiaries. To reject this proposal would set him at odds with the values, culture and identity of the organisation, which would raise his current stress level. As the only sensitive post in the company, the president's post was revocable ad *nutum*. I felt Arnaud's distress as he told me about his childhood spent far away from his parents at a very young age, having had to leave them when he was ten years old to attend secondary school. Life as a boarder at an early age must have developed survival qualities in this man, who had strongly cathected the values of work, competition and vigorous behaviour; it also revealed an affective fragility. Having mentioned the early years of his life spent far from his family, once the relationship of trust was established, he then told me about his way of fighting in life; he used the metaphor of combat sports such as judo, karate and aikido: "I really like aikido; it is not an aggressive sport, it is an evasive sport, a martial art in which the goal is to turn the aggression directed at you back on the other person ..."

Was he telling me here that he was going through a period of combat in which he was using the strategy of evasion? Arnaud then explained to me that the general management of the corporation had appointed another man to run the company while keeping him in his role; this man was his double–he was supervising all his decisions and their implementation. He could no longer tolerate this invisible presence and the threat that accompanied it. For over a year, Arnaud told no one about his grievances and torments. One year of daily aggression eroded his resistances and the worst came: myocardial infarction. He survived and, trusting in the future, decided that a new destiny awaited him; he placed himself in the hands of a "head-hunting" agency and found a post as president in a financial institution.

Commentary

Arnaud shared the common fate of "top managers" who are subjected to professional stress; the social environment is the main variable that enables us to elucidate operational processes in organisations and their consequences for human psychic and somatic health. Constant tensions and their conversion into quanta of excitations impose harsh ordeals on the psychic apparatus. The latency period is variable; it depends on the stability of the psychic processes, somatic resilience (degree of vulnerability to be assessed) and the intensity of the daily emotional shocks. We are still a long way from being able to formalise a problem that has so many unpredictable factors. The threat of losing power certainly arouses castration anxieties and fosters the onset of depressive phenomena mediated by feelings of distress (diffuse anxieties and, in all probability, essential depression) and a reactivation of past traumatic situations–leaving his parents at an early age. We can trace the fluctuations and floodings in psychic activity; isolated by his lack of communication with his family and dependent on the prevailing ideology ("only weak men complain"), Arnaud finally "cracked" at the end of a year in a form of "burn-out" or professional exhaustion. His mental representations of the martial arts helped him for a while (work of the preconscious) but his defences were eroded (reactivation of the weakened childhood–loss of parental love), throwing him into a phase of essential depression. The psychic apparatus temporarily ceased to function and the quantum of excitations suddenly moved from the psychic to the somatic level (decathexis), setting in motion the complex machinery of neurotransmitters.

The somatic disorder is therefore a manifestation of a bodily defence that secures the individual's survival. We can only briefly mention here the hypothesis of an archaic regression accompanied by a distressed state that is tantamount to imminent disappearance; the somatic processes have quickly taken over in order to ensure the continuity of life. My hypothesis is an alternation and conjunction of rapid phases of anomalies in mental functioning (in Marty's sense), followed by somatic disorders that show the progressive instigation of neurotransmitters and hormonal interplay as mentioned above. This leads to an exacerbation of somatic symptoms, with psychic equilibria moving through regressive phases until manifestations of narcissistic destabilisation appear ("am I still as good as I was at the start of my presidency?"), as the last defence and final stage before the heart attack and *above all the emergence of the narcissism of death.*

I never had sight of Arnaud's medical file, but we must consider his age (50+ years) if we are to complete the picture: *risk factors multiply over the course of time.*

Alice–"A female Ulysses" or "when the body gives way"

Alice was lying in her hospital bed and seemed to be suffering intensely–she mentioned a pain that had she had been experiencing incessantly for fifteen months and this problem remained latent throughout the examination. She had had an accident at work, falling down some stairs while carrying a package that she did not dare to drop in order to protect herself; she had fallen over backwards and slid on her back down a large number of steps. She had lain on the ground for a few minutes and had felt continual pains ever since. Why did this apparently ordinary accident take place? What part was played by the layout of the premises and what part by her frustrations and conflicts? These were the questions I was silently formulating.

"I didn't break anything; I had a thyroid operation two years ago and I have a cyst in my left breast that is under investigation". Alice was around 40 years old and had been married for over 20 years, with a 16-year-old daughter; she was a self-taught woman of action. She was an executive in a company based in the provinces and had worked there for nearly 20 years, moving up through all the grades; she seemed to have very much enjoyed her work, which she had strongly cathected and she travelled all over France, taking decisions. Because of her company's location, she had lived in a large provincial town until two years previously, meeting up with her husband, who had been living in Paris for over fifteen years. It was he who travelled back and forth between Paris and his country home. But she had then moved and was now living in a comfortable and beautiful flat in Paris, where she had accepted a less skilled post in a "fast-moving" company. What had happened? Why did she have this accident at work? What was she suffering from? I silently pondered these questions and wondered about *the relationship between this workplace accident and the mourning for a profession that she had strongly cathected.* What were the underlying difficulties that had caused this disturbance in the processes of adapting to a new situation? I have often noticed that patients have a different representation of their illness from doctors; I asked her what she was suffering from and she replied that she had had coccygodynia since her accident but *she saw herself as an invalid: she could no longer do the shopping and it was difficult to carry out household tasks.* She was suffering from laterosacral pains in her right side and scoliosis. (This is a further example I have encountered of an accident that comes at just the right time–but at what cost!)

I deeply sensed her distress and anxiety, as if all her physical confidence were disappearing and she could no longer rely on her body in any way. Alice's whole life up to this point had been based on motricity and on motor activities: travelling all year round, attending seminars and meetings; she conjured up a nomadic and geographically mobile life that gave her a great deal of fulfilment (and, I suppose, enjoyment). Suddenly this life had been interrupted and had given way to a sedentary lifestyle. She had settled back with her husband and found some work that was certainly active but less rewarding–this is how I reconstruct one thread of this patient's history, which is limited, as with many somatic patients, to the statement of actual events. Alice was like Ulysses, having returned home after a long journey in which events and action have predominated over emotional and imaginative forms of expression.

Commentary

An attack on motor functions and hormonal deregulation (thyroid operation) can herald the onset of more severe symptoms if a progressive disorganisation emerges. Alice had lost her work and her mobility: losing her work had reactivated her pathological mourning for her father, who had been replaced at the time by a dog that became her companion as a thirteen-year-old girl. At present she has some pedigree dogs who keep her company. However, her move to Paris resulted in separation from her mother and she thus lost the maternal protective-shield function that had supported her for nearly 20 years. This recent restriction of her physical activities put an end to a psychic economy based on excitational discharge in motricity and threw the patient into an objectal depressive phase accompanied by specific anxieties, which is a sign that psychic regression is not so deep and that it may be possible for a resumption of mental life to emerge after the depressive phase. It seems that there is a relative reorganisation, at least temporarily, in a hypochondriac mode and the patient is drawing some secondary benefits from the current illness. Alice presents the serious problem faced by action-orientated men and women who have based their psychic economy on motricity; I think she possesses adequate psychic resources for an imminent reorganisation. It seems in fact that the attack on her somatic functions has gone no further than physical activity; the hormonal deregulation has ceased, since the cyst in her breast has turned out to be benign, which in the opposite case would have indicated a progressive disorganisation affecting the genital organs. On the other hand, this accident has had consequences for this patient's sexual life, thus relating to the psychic dimension of the trauma, with the physical pain replacing the mental suffering. When subjectivity disappears by fits and starts during regressive phases, the body takes over and physical pain substitutes for the mental suffering. Alice found that the hospital environment fostered the disappearance of excitations induced by the various traumas. This protective shield role is one that is frequently played by the hospital setting.

Some research conducted in the 1980s emphasised the importance of psychological variables in endocrine diseases; in fact, researchers indicate that one of the first aspects of stimuli from stressful situations to induce an endocrine response is psychological in nature and that these most specifically involve the corticoadrenal axis (Mason, 1968). Unlike the approach adopted by Hans Selye, the originator of "stress", which implicates a non-specific response in the organism, more recent studies demonstrate that psychological factors are one of the explanatory variables in stress responses that activate the endocrine system. Earlier works on stress underestimated the common element in experiments on physical stimuli, since this involved exposing living organisms to new environments that were strange or rather unfamiliar. The psychological dimension gave a much fuller explanation of laboratory animals" responses to stressful situations than the specific physical trauma to which they had been exposed. The experiments demonstrated that when the animals were exposed to stimuli in such a way that they did not experience these as distressing experiences or new situations, typical stressors such as heat or food deprivation did not activate the pituitary-adrenal system. The concept that psychological variables can activate or inhibit the endocrine system has since received further support from experiments conducted on both animals and human beings.

This new model incorporating the psychological variable should not make us neglect the somatic aspect, since the stress response that can be defined as a symptom comprises many changes in neurochemical and metabolic processes. There are findings that clearly prove that all the hormones in the endocrine system–catecholamines, insulin, growth hormone and prolactin–can be influenced by psychological factors. Moreover, it has been demonstrated that endorphins are acutely sensitive to stress; in fact, it appears that almost all stimuli capable of instigating an adrenocorticotrophic hormone response in the pituitary gland can also release beta-endorphins into the bloodstream (Guillemin et al., 1977). There are two reasons for the emphasis placed in this research on the pituitary-adrenal axis in the context of so-called "psychosomatic" illnesses; one is the creation of extensive databases to analyse the effects of psychological variables on the pituitary-adrenal system; the other is the profound impact that adrenal hormones have on the life functions associated with general health.

On the basis of these few observations, I would like to qualify my approach by suggesting that there are appropriate bodily responses to every stimulus in both psychic and somatic terms, in a complex interrelation in which activation and inhibition are processes constantly at work.

Sandrine–confronted with destructive drives

Sandrine was a 39-year-old woman whose manner was defensive as she faced me; she was on her guard. She had told the departmental intern that she did not want to see a psychologist. Her reasons became clear when it emerged that she had been diagnosed with conversion hysteria three years earlier in another department of the hospital, which had left her with some very bad memories. This reveals the unintended consequences of stating or communicating diagnoses that then generate reinforcements of psychic defence mechanisms. Moreover, every time she consulted a doctor about her backache, she was invariably told that it was psychological, which emphasised the medical intuition of psychogenic disturbances but caused a narcissistic injury in the process, since this momentarily deprived the patient of a means of somatic defence (body image).

Before embarking on any examination, I felt that I first needed to establish a relationship of trust; I decided to do no more than listen in a kindly way, conveying understanding and warmth. Having looked at me as if to assess my sincerity, Sandrine talked to me: she had had a series of operations over the past five years–total hysterectomy, thyroid gland and, in the last two years, disc operations. I asked her what could have happened to make her health deteriorate like that, with four operations in five years. Her first thought was a primary trauma: when she was 33 years old, her husband had separated from her (another woman) and she had been left alone with her two daughters, one aged nineteen and the other aged seven; her misfortune was then compounded when she was made redundant for economic reasons. The factory in which she was a senior manager closed down. She had started working at a very early age and had had a child when she was seventeen years old: a mistake, she said, looking at me as if she was expecting a response from me in an emerging transference relationship. I vaguely sensed a wish for narcissistic reassurance and parental approval, so I complimented her and congratulated her on having a young daughter at her side when she was so young herself. I was considering deeply what I was saying. She then became livelier again and her confidence returned. She was the eldest of five siblings born at one-year intervals. She had had to take care of her brothers and sisters when she was very young and this had left her with some very bad memories, as had her alcoholic father who had died ten years earlier and had beaten her mother, who had sought comfort elsewhere. Altogether, she had had a painful and unfulfilling childhood and youth.

It appeared that she had wanted to escape from her family environment by taking refuge in marriage, only to find a husband who turned out to be alcoholic like her father! *Once again, we encounter the eternal recurrence of the repetition compulsion.* These hardships imposed a heavy burden on a fragile psychosomatic organisation and gave rise to the essential depression that I hypothesised following her separation from her husband, since a few months later (progressive disorganisation) she had had her first operation, followed by others since this time. How much longer would this continue? What are the stages of the fixations that can slow and halt this impulse? With patients undergoing disorganisation who are strongly integrated in the present and lack connections between the past, present and future, the prognosis is suspended. I wanted to know if she had any hopes and I asked about her plans for after she left hospital: how was she thinking of getting back on her feet? She replied that she did have some plans–she wanted to become a secretary and train for a new profession. She thought that the sedentary position would alleviate the pain caused by her discal hernias and would be preferable to her previous work at the factory in which she had had to stand–she was taking some typing classes. She was optimistic because she thought that she would be able to find work in her home town. She then talked to me about the medicines–antidepressants, tranquillisers and so on–that she had been taking for five years. She wanted to lower the doses and eventually stop taking them altogether. She was afraid both of their effects and of the withdrawal process but considered it necessary. Through this request, she was seeking to overturn the superegoic injunctions of a doctor from her previous period in hospital, who had forced her to take antidepressants; she wanted this obligation to be removed and for her new choice of professional career to be approved. I complimented her once again on her professional plans, asked her to consult a practitioner about the medicines she was taking and strongly encouraged her to pursue her endeavours. She smiled at me as if some inner tension had been eased. She seemed to trust me completely and she confirmed my impression by expressing a wish to see me again the following week. At the end of the session, the emerging resumption of life instincts that would be accompanied by a reorganising impulse was clear to see; this was a sign that a point of fixation had been reached that was stable enough to reactivate an impulse of psychic resumption.

Commentary

"In mental neuroses, trauma is resolved in the internal elaborative processes at the level of the subject's mental activity, as well as in the production of symptoms. In character neuroses ... when regressive organisations do not prove stable enough, there can be no internal elaboration of the trauma. A disorganisation of the mental apparatus itself then emerges" (Marty, 1976, p. 109). Sandrine is the living illustration of this transition from psychic malfunctioning to the disorganisation of somatic functions, with a resumption of a progredient impulse. This is not a case of conversion hysteria but *a poorly mentalised character neurosis*, the structure of which has rapidly been flooded by the accumulation of excitations induced by the many close-set and constant traumas, activating the above-mentioned hormonal system. The organisation of bio-regulation has taken over by restricting the severity of the disorders as far as possible, since the objective pursued by the body is to ensure survival, except where destructive forces prevent the fundamental objective from being achieved, as we will see in the next chapter.

Emma–confronted with a new challenge, or surplus weight problems

Emma was 1.67 m tall and weighed 95 kg. She was an accomplished sportswoman, playing handball, combat sports such as karate and aggressive sports such as American boxing, a sport that allows close-up fighting and blows that cannot be struck in karate, in which there is greater control. At the time of our interview, Emma was playing goalkeeper in handball but because of her weight but she had recently been dropped from her team because she could not move around quickly. She gave no indication during the interview that giving up the sport had caused her any mental anguish; she compensated for this frustration by practising other sports and activities in which she wanted to show and prove to others that she was still up to the mark. She told me that she been out for a ride with one of her mountain-biking friends but had pedalled normally until her friend started whistling at her because she could no longer keep up; Emma could thereby prove to herself in a narcissistic way that she still measured up but she also revealed the expression of these aggressive impulses. She looked sporty, with broad shoulders and walked in a way that suggested great physical power. She carried a sports bag and seemed relaxed in our interview.

It had all started six years earlier; her mother had had an accident while carrying a bowl of boiling water and for a few months Emma had tended her mother's wounds (why had she been so affected by this accident? Reactivation of the oedipal conflict). This care, which she said she had taken over from a nurse, had greatly restricted her activities.

I thought about her proximity to her mother and her possible unresolved rivalry and her hostility that had never manifested. She had thus had to take on too many tasks, overloading her schedule. Shortly afterwards, in October, on returning to her flat she had looked through the window of her building and seen a man hanging from a tree in the garden of the neighbouring house. It was one of her childhood friends; this gave her such a shock that she spent the next two months in a state of sideration. She had no memories from this period. She thought that she had very recently mourned this friend. Who was he for her? What was the impact of this trauma?

Emma still kept up with all her childhood friends; she lived in the middle of one of the housing estates in this suburb. She knew everyone; she had been at school with all the children in the neighbourhood. The people seemed to have known each other over several generations. After describing this ordeal, she told me about her break-up with a young man with whom she had lived for two years. Her parents had established the young couple in a house adjoining theirs that had belonged to Emma's paternal grandmother who had died a few years earlier. Emma had loved her grandmother very much. Her grandmother was at the origin of her "family romance": she had told her that her father was not her real father because she did not have the same colour hair as her parents! (Once again, the oedipal avoidance appears in the anamnestic report).

She had met her boyfriend while snowboarding at the foot of a ski run. He was a tall, sporty man who came from a middle-class family. Laughing, she told me that she was stronger than him (again this "tomboy" aspect came out). It seemed that the boyfriend's father had fully accepted her but the mother had not and when the marriage plans advanced the mother asked her son to draw up a marriage contract; it was then noticed that Emma also had some money. Her boyfriend wanted to have a child; she was studying and did not want to sacrifice her career. They separated shortly afterwards (possible rejection of motherhood concealed behind professional reasons). At the end of the interview, I made reference to her desire for a child in order to assess the feminine component of her identity and one of the possible roles being played by the obesity! She talked to me about her boyfriend as a romantic love from which she had now recovered. She had lived in a sort of romantic illusion. Since this time, she had had some boyfriends with whom she had affairs from time to time without forming any attachment. It was the same with another of her childhood friends whom she met now and then. Emma seemed to have remained stuck in adolescent relations.

Emma had a motorbike that she loved. However, she had recently had an accident in which she had been trapped for a while underneath

its 300 kg weight. To conclude this series of traumatic events of varying intensity, she told me about her recent fight with a neighbour
who was a drug-addict. He had tried to attack Emma and her mother with a knife. Emma had defended herself and mentioned for the
first time her ability to kill at one blow. She had suddenly been
afraid of the power of her own physical strength. She had mentioned this possibility to the policemen who came to their rescue and
they told her there was no reason to reproach herself.

Emma talked to me about her relations with her parents, whom
she loved very much; breast-fed (for a few months), she was then
encouraged from the age of two and a half years old to play sport by
her mother, who was a sportswoman. Since this time, she had played
sport for between a few hours and 40 hours per week. At the sports
centre, she pursued this intensive training. She never showed any
reservations or criticisms with regard to this particular relationship.
This sports practice seemed to be the source of the greatest possible
pleasure. This was her world view and it constituted the outlet for
her somatic and libidinal energy discharges. *I am referring to a form of
auto-erotic pleasure that was sought from the earliest age–an indication of
a probable sensorimotor fixation at an archaic stage of her development.*

Emma told me about her father; a tall, thin man who was ten
kilograms underweight, as she had been before putting on weight
(emergence of a defensive impulse against an oedipal connection).
Her father had been retired for six years; he had become intolerable,
drinking and smoking almost two packets of cigarettes a day. Once
again here, I had the strange sense of an alexithymic individual,
someone who felt no emotion, who either did not have emotions or
repressed them–I was not immediately certain which.

Emma returned to the subject of her weight and the hurtful criticisms made by some of her friends or by shop assistants. She had
even broken the mirrors in her house in order to discharge tensions
and frustrations. Recently, she had begun to look at herself again in a
full-length mirror. She was also wearing make-up (I interpreted this
form of narcissistic resumption as a positive sign and, as on some
previous occasions when observing obese people, I noted to myself
the discrimination to which they are subjected in our society).

I asked Emma some questions relating to her self-image: how did
she regard her obesity? How did she hold her own with other people
and manage to confront them? Did she see her weight as a carapace,

a kind of defensive armour? (What was Emma protecting herself from? From internal drive attacks, external dangers, or both?) Was she drawing any benefit from her weight? Was her weight perhaps an unconscious bodily response to the extreme intensity of her sports training? She told me that this same view had been expressed in a slightly different way by a doctor who said that her body might have used up all its reserves and that everything she ingested was being put immediately into store!

What are we to make of someone who has spent more than a quarter-century cathecting her muscles and motor activities? This involves a narcissistic cathexis and an auto-erotic pleasure that seem to predominate in physical activity, *as if Emma were self-sufficient*. The other aspect of her personality is the fundamental question of her sexual identity; I think that this identity was not yet psychically established and that she developed behaviours that appeared to suggest satisfactory heterosexual relations had been established. I suspect that this was in fact an oedipal defensive behaviour in the guise of social conformity; she wanted to show that she was like other people. This is connected with a mental attitude in her parents during the pregnancy that gave birth to Emma; her mother had been expecting a boy to be born because of the energetic kicking from the foetus. The doctor had interpreted this as the activity of a boy. Emma therefore grew up in a family setting that was ambivalent about her sexual identity. As a child, until the age of six years old, Emma had worn little dresses, which she happily discarded as soon as she started at primary school in favour of shorts and later sports trousers. Only a course of psychotherapy would provide more information about the mother's unconscious mental state.

What must be accepted, however, is the privileged mode of discharge of tensions exclusively in muscular activity and acting out. The psychic apparatus is inhibited in this type of functioning–with an avoidance of representations and an oral fixation reinforced very early by the expenditure of energy in various sports activities. Surplus weight and later obesity, if it develops, are stages on the long road leading to the most severe metabolic problems: diabetes, accompanied by a series of somatic disorganisations. This type of functioning could be intensely disabling if Emma came to regard her muscular activity as decelerated or disturbed; for the time being, she has not developed any other recourses. This is a neurosis with

uncertain mentalisation accompanied by the inhibition of representations.

Emma was confronted with a twofold problem: the early cathexis
of bodily motricity and the question of her sexual identity; moreover, the lack of conflict with her parents during adolescence had led
to a massive cathexis of libidinal and aggressive drives towards
combat sports. This drive orientation was at the origin of her rival-
rous behaviour with boys, as revealed by certain incidents such as
her comment about her ex-fiancé–"I am stronger than him". Emma
has remained stuck in a position of oedipal rivalry with her father
and therefore hypercathexis of the active drives; the narcissistic-
phallic fixation is clearly identifiable. She has yet to embark on the
path of access to female identity.

There are several possible hypotheses to explain not the bodily
takeover of psychic problematics but, in this particular case, the use
of the body as an object of physical defence–defensive armour–and
symbolic psychic defence–unconsciously no longer pleasing her
father. Hypotheses:

1. An early predilection for sporting activities and an uncertainty
    surrounding her sexual identity from the outset of life (a boy
    having been wanted).

2. A succession of traumas that rapidly jeopardised the patient's
    fragile psychic and metabolic equilibrium, gradually leading to
    weight gain as a form of self-defence against both external exci-
    tations (traumas) and internal excitations (drive manifestations).
    Emma protects herself (defensive armour, carapace, etc.) with
    her body against adversity and against a connection with her
    father. Her love affair, which might have indicated the change of
    object from the mother towards the father, was not fulfilled; she
    has remained stuck in a defensive phallic position. We can
    clearly observe the lack of psychic defences, which are put on
    hold because of this hypercathexis of the body (anomalies in
    mental functioning).

3. The emotional shocks associated with the successive traumas
    have given rise to the disequilibrium in the patient's energy and
    metabolism. The classical equation of the energy equilibrium
    (modification of energy reserves = absorption of energy
    [AE]–expenditure of energy [EE]) has furthered the understanding

of human obesity, but also introduced some uncertainties that have been elucidated by Alpert (1990). Alpert demonstrated that when energy stores are modified, the classical equation of energy equilibrium no longer applies to living organisms because it is static. Using a new dynamic equation, Alpert showed that modifications in energy reserves are time-dependent and limited. In fact, an initial slight disequilibrium of energy in the positive direction cannot produce a very great increase in body weight. Alpert considers it unlikely that the origin of obesity lies in differences between energy supply and expenditure; *rather, it proceeds from a chronic dynamic disequilibrium between energy supply and expenditure* (Ravussin & Swinburn, 1992). It is this remark that I will take into consideration since, according to the hypotheses developed throughout this work, transmission of quantities of excitations from the psychic to the somatic sphere by means of the (coenaesthetic) organisation of bio-regulation introduces a dynamic and often permanent disturbance in somatic equilibria–in this particular case, energy equilibria.

Another factor of disequilibrium in the somatic processes must be taken into consideration, namely the information provided by leptin to the hypothalamus concerning the state of the adipocytal reserves, inducing metabolic and nutritional responses that seek to maintain homeostasis in the fat stores. Some recent works (mid-1990s) on the role of genetics in obesity (Clément, Basdevant, Guy-Grand & Froguel, 1977) have emphasised the *ob* gene, specifically expressed in adipocytes in mice and human beings. It produces leptin, the circulating hormone from the cytokine group, which interacts with specific receptors, particularly those in the central nervous system. "All these works concur with regard to the multiple physiological effects of leptin, which influence not only alimentary uptake (still to be demonstrated in human beings) and thermogenesis but probably also the glucidic metabolism (regulating the secretion and cellular interaction of insulin), as well as the reproductive functions".

All these studies with their promising results must give consideration to the psychological dimension in the context of the therapies proposed; in fact, a psychotherapy for obese patients, through a resumption of psychic activity, will have major repercussions on the return to an equilibrium that is both psychic and somatic. A new psychosomatic equilibrium will be established and it will be possible to ascertain that this new equilibrium will not be a return to the initial conditions. In the above-mentioned case and in many other cases of obesity that I have observed, there are many suitable therapies that can help a patient to reduce his weight, though rarely to return to his original weight. However, another steady state of somatic and psychic energy equilibrium can be attained.

All the medical and psychosomatic research refers to possible advances in the treatment of obesity based on the understanding of factors that regulate human body weight. They mention in particular the discovery of events that affect the centres of equilibrium that regulate body weight; they emphasise the following different factors: physical exercise, appetite-regulating medication, surgical procedures to reduce stomach size, intragastic balloons, methods of dietary adjustment and so on as factors that affect the equilibrium centres of the weight.

None of these research studies refers to changes that may be brought about by psychotherapy, which might also in fact be able to influence the centres of equilibrium, as I have sought to suggest above in the general case description. *It will not be possible to achieve any return to equilibrium without the participation of the psychic apparatus.*

Appendix

Here I shall demonstrate the application of "psychosomatic classification" (Marty & Stora, 1988) to the observation of Amanda; after Pierre Marty's death in 1993, I developed the classification, which led to a new psychosomatic classification in 2005.

Structure

• character neurosis with uncertain mentalisation.

Main frequent characteristics

• objectal anxieties–alarm signals accompanied by representational bindings.

Character traits

• Oral (fixations)–alcoholism and tobacco addiction–use of modes of oral discharge favoured for over ten years;

• Phallic-narcissistic–professional success and the desire to obtain diplomas to assist career progression–acquisition of a professional phallus in the banking sector;

• Sado-masochistic–eroticised relations, both physical and mental–the relations with her father to whose violence she has been subjected since childhood without any aggressive response on her part, thus relations to which she has passively submitted (not forgetting the reinforcement of masochistic pleasure derived from such a situation); but this relational erotisation has resulted in an oral pregenital fixation. Failure to establish the oedipal organisation.

• Inhibition, avoidance or suppression of representations and thoughts–in the guise of statements of actual and past events; it seems possible at first that the patient has a rich and fluid mentalisation but certain zones do not seem to be psychically cathected and do not form the object of representations.

• Suppression of drive expressions in activity–this is the most important point–when confronted with changes and traumas giving rise to a surplus of excitations that is not taken up by the psychic apparatus, the patient finds herself incapable of mental elaboration, with the result that the excitations find an outlet at the bodily level because the mental pathway is closed. Having strongly cathected physical activity as a favoured mode of psychic regulation of excitations (tensions and frustrations), this patient finds herself deprived of locomotor exercise through the suppression of this mode, with severe consequences that lead to organic symptoms.

• Severe anomalies in mental functioning.

Main characteristics in terms of the interpretation

• Artistic sublimations–these are blocked by her giving up the piano and replacing it with gymnastics, thereby reinforcing the libidinal cathexis of the body;

• Family sexual trauma connected with the father's sadism, impeding the patient's sexual development.

Main characteristics in terms of the anamnesis

• Non-hysterical conversions–hysterical affinities; that is, the complaint from which the patient is suffering is not an object of erotisation and has no symbolic meaning.

• Pre-existing unresolved mourning–pathological mourning for her father, as well as the loss of her children who left her, leading to the current medical problems.

• Problems in mother-child relations in her first two years of life–the patient's mother having to take care of two-year-old twins when the patient was born as a child who, as mentioned above, was not wanted.

• Significant pre-pubertal change in the relational economy–leaving the family home as an adolescent in order to work and lead an independent life–she is not very forthcoming about this crucial period.

• Acute or subacute depressions–symptomatic in the psychoanalytic sense, following the mourning for her father and separation from both her children.

• Some doubt concerning the essential depression–it is entirely possible that the patient is going through a phase of essential depression but her hospitalisation may have put an end to the process by reawakening her life instincts.

Serial operations

- Suicide attempts–two suicide attempts before the current illness, which seems to be the best possible solution in terms of confronting her problems.

- Habitual drug addictions–the patient concealed her recourse to tobacco and alcohol by omission but these two dependencies, revealing the patient's oral fixation, have been an outlet for more than ten years for evacuating the surplus tensions. I obtained this information from her medical file. It may also mean that deprivation of her drug addictions has led to the patient's range of possibilities for discharge of tensions being reduced to the soma.

Main current characteristics

- Essential depression–disguised by her return to hospital? Did she not state that only fifteen days earlier she had been thinking of committing suicide?

- Progressive disorganisation halted by a point of somatic fixation: current illness accompanied by pains, "pain can constitute an object of affective cathexis to which the subject becomes attached and ultimately can substitute for a lost object" (Marty, 1976).

- Recent loss of a significant object; unresolved mourning; loss of her second son, who has left her for his father.

- Recent sexual difficulties.

- Recent restrictions of physical activities.

- Frustration of sexual pleasure.

CHAPTER FOUR

Adrienne and Sanjay–progressive disorganisation and somatisations: the emergence of irreversible unstable equilibria

"Life may want to abandon me, but I shall never abandon it".

A female patient

Doctors and patients confronted with cancer

"In the hospital, at the end of the corridor with pale green walls that seem to be telling patients to have hope, but not too much, waits the cancer specialist, courteous and elegant, wearing a discreet tie and polished shoes" (1994, p. 23.) This is how a patient who had six years of treatment for a breast tumour describes her encounter with the doctor who has been overseeing her care throughout these years, whom she is returning to see for a routine check, believing that it is her last visit to the hospital. Trusting and cautious, she is then told by her doctor, who studies the chest X-ray, to see a radiologist again, which ultimately leads to the removal of the upper left lobe of her lung. This patient, the heroine of Élisabeth Gille's novel, *Le crabe sur la banquette arrière* [The crab on the back bench], tells us her observations and thoughts in an impersonal and distant way that seems to caricature this medical universe that she will be inhabiting for the duration of her terrible illness. The patient, whose forename and surname are never revealed, conveys to us the fears and distress that she feels when confronted with the doctors' aloof and distant attitude. Her literary style appears simply to be reflecting this particular doctor-patient relationship, which belongs to a specific culture and civilisation.

At the outset of this chapter on cancer and autoimmune diseases, I think it is important to address, albeit briefly, this painful experience to which both patients and their doctors are subjected. *Patients' lives are totally shattered by hearing that they have the illness* and doctors, whose training does not prepare them for this encounter, adopt several attitudes, principally resorting to technical discourse to protect themselves from the surplus of emotional flooding experienced by patients in connection with this information or, all too often, lack of information. Here I should like to discuss a crucial question: should the doctor always communicate his diagnosis to the patient? And if he does so, what form should this take? Should this kind of communication not form part of medical training?

As we will be able to observe, in practice doctors are often unprepared for this relationship and they do not ask for help from qualified psychologists, psychoanalysts or psychosomaticians who would be able to provide some valuable assistance.

What does the doctor say to Gille's heroine in this encounter? The patient having stated that all her tests have remained completely normal, the doctor does not refer to metastases or the spread of the cancer, but says: "There is just one small thing there that does not seem to me to fit with what you are saying. So go back to see your radiologist" ... When the patient asks the radiologist if he has seen something, he replies: "Oh no, nothing at all. It's good, very good. No problem, none at all, except possibly a minute inflammation in the left vertex. What do you expect, with your two packs of cigarettes a day?" (p. 24). The results follow, with medical commentaries that are incomprehensible to the layperson but lead the patient to conclude that it is impossible to get the truth from a radiologist, as she remembers experiencing the same scenario six years earlier. She then goes to see a surgeon to learn more about the diagnosis that is still unknown to her and this conversation with the surgeon has an unreal quality: "Good, well, yes, if that suits you I'll operate on the 2nd", to which the patient replies, "Yes, doctor, but on what?" The surgeon says: "But on your cancer of course". The patient, who is uncertain about the diagnosis, is then told by the doctor: "There"s no doubt about that; what did you suppose? But don't worry; nowadays, fifty percent of them are cured" (p. 24). The patient, who is not lacking in humour (and uses it to protect herself from this emotional shock), then thinks about the fifty percent that are not cured!

It is obvious that the doctor-patient relationship is unsatisfactory here and that for both parties it is a source of traumatic stress, accompanied by anxiety, fear and suffering. Doctors cannot afford to ignore the emotional dimension of this severe illness, which entails a deep sense of abandonment at a basic level. A fundamental change in working practices should be considered as a matter of urgency.

Psychosomatic approaches

The above observation is supported by findings in psychosomatic medical research (Haynal & Pasini, 1984).

1. The progress of the illness is likely to be influenced by the subject's personality, his psychic resistance or his resignation and the renunciation that follows from this.

2. *The prognosis is improved by maintaining communication between doctor and patient, which saves the patient from feeling abandoned.*

Cancer therefore constitutes a psychological ordeal for the patient, his family and the care team; in the light of these observations, it is strongly advisable to provide both patients and doctors with some psychological assistance.

The psychosomatic approach to cancer patients, with its psychotherapeutic and theoretical dimensions, differs from other medicine in that its clinical approach, as we have seen in the previous chapters, is characterised by empathy for the patient in a constant concern to give support, which is not a substitute for medical treatment with chemotherapy or radiotherapy.

All the observations from Galen to the present day, particularly in the United States, concur that there is a connection between cancer and specific emotional states. According to Galen, women with a depressive temperament showed a predisposition towards this illness. Without citing all the literature in this field, let us take the example of Nunn, who stated in a work entitled *Cancer of the Breast* in 1822 that emotional factors influenced the growth of tumours. The personality profiles used by specialists, especially in North America, as possible but uncertain indicators of cancer constitute only one element of the diagnosis and do not provide the basis for any definite or firm conclusions; they simply use certain psychological characteristics that belong, as we will see below, to a more general picture of psychic functioning.

Pierre Marty's contribution to the study of severe somatisations will initially help to formulate the different stages of the first model that I shall be using as an underlying framework of the theoretical approach adopted here. The impulses of progressive disorganisation (Marty, 1990, pp. 31–32)[18] that lead to a severe illness conform to the following pattern:

- Accumulation of excitations at the psycho-affective level, with no possibility of mental elaboration and reduced possibilities of behavioural discharge;

- More or less rapid mental disorganisation, depending on the size of the network of associations of ideas;

- Essential depression (Marty, 1990, p. 29)[19]–resumption of a type of childhood depression or a latent depression) and sometimes operative life (Marty, 1990, p. 27);[20]

- Diffuse anxiety indicating the subject's state of psychosomatic distress;

- Somatic disorganisation originating from outbreaks of various illnesses–or illnesses with fits that may constitute the first somatic symptoms of a progressive disorganisation;

- Finally, the emergence of a severe progressive illness (cardiovascular disease, autoimmune diseases and cancers).

These severe illnesses can be more or less slow to emerge, depending on the latency period and the subject in question.

In May 1986, Pierre Marty sent a memorandum to some other colleagues and me, proposing for our weekly discussion *a list of criteria that apply to a subject suffering from a severe illness*. The list is as follows: *diffuse anxiety, masochistic appearance of the "destiny neurosis" type with inadequate integration of passive satisfactions, latent depression, predominant ideal ego, conscious or unconscious rejection of regressions, mourning for individuals or loss of objects that were directly or indirectly significant during the mother's pregnancy or the first two years of life, frequent essential depressions, outbreaks of illnesses, current essential depression, progressive disorganisation, operative life, a change in the relational economy within the preceding year.*

This hypothesis, which Pierre Marty described as "maximal", has not been confirmed by my research (1995) because of the small sample that I had available at that time. However, my research did produce some significant results that were statistically validated. I found three significant characteristics and features, namely: *essential depressions, progressive disorganisation and diffuse anxieties.*

This certainly does not mean that any causal relationship has been established between cancer and certain psychological factors, but the presence of these three factors among patients suffering from breast cancer has been statistically proven.

This raises the question as to whether such findings apply to every type of cancer. In conclusion to my research on the relationships between mental organisations and somatic illnesses based on Marty's theoretical approach, I explain in my article that his hypotheses concerning the connections between the degree of mentalisation of neuroses and somatic illnesses could not as yet be confirmed.

Over the course of 70 years in Europe, we have moved in psychosomatic medicine from an approach based on determining disease profiles that emphasise behaviours to a psychosomatic psychoanalytic approach (primarily developed by the French), recently amplified by an approach based on psychoneuroimmunomodulation. In fact, in the early 1990s it was discovered that the immune system interacts with the endocrine glands and the nervous system. This gave rise to a new discipline, psychoneuroimmunology, to account for the relations between severe psycho-affective shocks and the onset of autoimmune diseases or the connections between hormonal injections (thyroid and adrenal cortex) and the resulting immune responses. An explanation is emerging for the molecular basis of these interactions but not as yet the psychic dimension; we have yet to go beyond the neuronal foundation of these interrelations.

Before embarking on a clinical case description, I think it is important to respond to a final set of questions concerning *the latency period of a cancer.* In fact, the observations of some psychoanalyst-psychosomaticians frequently attest an onset of cancer in a six- to twelve-month period following mourning for a loved one, which is a hypothesis that requires testing.

Oncogenesis and the latency period—or how does the body produce a cancer and how long does this process take?

When a person is confronted with cancer, he asks himself a number of questions that correspond with the tacit thoughts of those who are treating him, although they rarely express these to their patients. Why me? When did this cancer begin? Is it recent? Does it date back further? Is it due to my family heredity? To my diet? My living habits? And so on. Anxiety and depression loom large and it is our responsibility to support people in this situation and answer their questions. It is clear that the first question is the most difficult to answer and it is the starting-point for many reflections. For the others, I prefer to refer briefly to molecular biology, which provides some satisfactory answers. The answers to these questions are silently present in the thoughts of every cancer specialist as he examines a patient who has come to consult him.

The human body is composed of around 60,000 billion cells, 200 billion of which die every day; regulation processes must ensure that every lost cell is replaced by a new cell with the same function in the same position; this is how cancerologists start to explain this universe of normal cells and cancer cells. In fact, the complex regulatory systems originate from the cell genome, which controls all the cellular activities.

Researchers have gradually revealed the risks of cellular malfunctioning, accounting for the molecular processes of cancerogenesis (fast-acting viruses, slow-acting viruses, oncogeneses and proto-oncogeneses). The discovery of proto-oncogenes in normal cells, almost identical to viral genes, has explained the deep deregulation or disorder that they institute in the organism when they elude the normal controls of cellular regulation; in one sense, these genes are potentially fatal for human beings.

There are various mechanisms that activate oncogenes, which might suggest that the genome is particularly vulnerable; however, the presence of a single oncogene is not enough to cancerise a cell:

cancerisation, if it occurs, takes place through successive stages. Professor Tubiana adds: "For a cancer to develop, other abnormalities in the genome are necessary, as well as *an immunodepression in the organism that enables neoplastic cells to multiply*" (1994, p. 58).

Some other information must be borne in mind when we are confronted with cancer, namely the characteristics of the cancer cell and the differing time-spans between initiation and onset of the cancer. A normal cell is mortal ("death is programmed and this is one of the characteristics of the cell under consideration"), whereas "one of the first stages of cancerisation is the lifting of this prohibition, which is termed "immortalisation"" (Tubiana, 1994, p. 58). The killer cells are immortal, as it were; normal cells multiply only when they receive the instruction, whereas cancer cells multiply at their own pace and steadily increase in number to form two types of tumour: benign tumours that never infiltrate the adjoining tissues and malignant tumours that invade other areas of tissue; this infiltration and migration activity is a characteristic of cancer cells and gives rise to metastases. Cancers develop at different rates; some grow only very slowly, while others display rapid, even meteoric, growth. However, it is important to bear in mind some considerations that will be useful for identifying when cancers originate and emerge:

1. All tumour cells stem from a single "transformed" cell that has passed its characteristics on to its descendants.

2. Periods ranging from 10 to 30 years elapse between the activation of the carcinogenic agent and the emergence of the cancer as a clinical entity.

3. The growth of the primitive tumour or metastases is steady and exponential; the average growth rate corresponds to a two-month doubling, but it varies greatly from one tumour to the next.

4. *When the tumour reaches a detectable size, a hidden period of seven to eight years has preceded its clinical emergence.*

5. Metastases are detectable only several years after the primitive tumour has been destroyed, because the doubling period means that there must be approximately a five-year interval before a detectable size is reached.

6. A five-year interval is generally allowed before there is any
    mention of a cure; in fact, this involves an average period calcu-
    lated on the basis of a doubling every other month correspon-
    ding to 30 doubling periods to reach the size of a tumour that is
    clinically or radiologically detectable. As the doubling period
    varies from one tumour to another, the range of recurrence can
    vary from five to 20 years, with 30 years after the initial treat-
    ment at the extreme end of the scale, which corresponds to a
    one-year doubling period.

7. The probability of the existence of metastases when the primi-
    tive tumour is being treated is connected with its volume: dur-
    ing the preliminary investigations, every practitioner and
    patient must bear in mind the period of clinical emergence of
    the cancer. I kept this consideration in mind when I met
    Adrienne.

Adrienne, or the scar of abandonment

I had discussed this patient with one of the clinical directors a week
earlier and this doctor, who was highly sensitive to psychological
characteristics of patients in the department, was contemplating
some questions about a cancer patient.

In accordance with my usual practice, I did not consult the
medical file and I went directly to this patient's room–she was not
there because the nurses had taken her to her radiotherapy session.
Adrienne was suffering from a malignant melanoma.

I waited a few minutes and she appeared on her stretcher, smiling and looking serene, with a specific expression that I was only
able to interpret later.

I looked at her before I started to speak, as if to reassure both her
and myself. I felt slightly at a loss; a psychoanalyst-psychosomatician
in a white coat is certainly more directly involved in the relationship
than a consultant psychoanalyst, who can preserve a
certain distance. What is the best way to proceed at a patient's bedside? Since the patient's first perception in the relationship involves
some confusion about the observer's identity (the patient usually
thinks in terms of a doctor's visit), I addressed this perception by first
asking about her illness: what are you suffering from? "A cancer, I

have two cancerous vertebrae; I also have some nodules, but the doctors told me that it has not spread and I would certainly like to believe them". I looked at her again and told her I was a psychosomatician and she seemed to know instinctively what that meant: someone you can talk to about your illness and your suffering. This put me in mind of Elisabeth Kübler-Ross's observation (1995) that when patients are trying to convey to you their perception of a terminal illness or any other tragedy, they use several languages. The first kind is clear language; as she explains, the patients who tell you "I know I've got cancer; I'm never going to leave this hospital' are those whom you will truly be able to help precisely because they help you–you will be able to have a dialogue with them because they make the task easy for you. Patients who are in the terminal phase and speak directly about their cancer have already transcended their fear of death; these patients ultimately help you. She adds that by contrast the patients who most desperately need your help are those who are in a shocked and stunned state. Adrienne belonged in this latter category. She said: "You know, I'm feeling all right, I'm not in pain, I'm being given morphine and that takes away the fears. People think about what's hurting you and I'm not hurting; I haven't had many changes in my life. I've been alone for 20 years, ever since my husband left me (a silence, then she continued). Twenty-one years ago life was happy, with two children ... Then suddenly my life broke in two ..."

She cried several times and it was painful to observe her expression as she looked at me, which seemed to evoke some long-distant plea, possibly that of a young girl or child asking for her mother's attention and affection. After this empathic, affective contact, this mental and affective connection, she resumed her story: "My husband left me and the evening before he went I still hadn't known he was going; he left with a woman who was younger than me (she said this without resentment or bitterness, as if she had mourned this, or alternatively revealing her inability to protect herself from such an adversity, her lack of aggression) ... I made two suicide attempts at that time. It took me six years to recover, including financially, I don't have a profession and I've been left with nothing'–"With nothing!" She continued: "He supports me, he gives me an allowance, but it's unofficial and we're still married". Instead of telling me, "I've suffered a lot", she said: "I was ill for six years and I was in a nursing home for seven weeks".

During our interview, she frequently confused times and periods of time; she was afraid that I wouldn't follow and that it was too confused ... but this temporal confusion raised a problem: was this forgetting due to repression or did it have a somatic cause? Were there metastases in the brain that were disturbing its functioning? These temporal confusions did not seem to bear the hallmark of repression. I kept this observation in mind for a later discussion with the doctor in order to suggest to him a more thorough medical examination.

"I've got two sons and two lovely daughters who have helped me a lot; I have a ten-year-old grandson (tears ...) I was in a nursing home and a psychiatrist I knew there has stayed in close touch with me ever since; I left her (or she left me, once again the trauma of abandonment) at the end of last year and my illness was thought to be due to the separation from the psychiatrist and I thought so too ... She's dropping me ... I've had backache for five months". Two of Adrienne's vertebrae were affected–and I thought to myself: the psychiatrist is no longer supporting her, but this lack of bodily support must have reawakened in Adrienne the lack of early support experienced by a child who was rarely taken into someone's arms! This thought strongly suggested itself to me from clinical experience and the immediate transference relationship.

"My mother left me when I was born because she was already old (38 years) and she didn't want a child. I found that hard to tolerate. I know that my parents weren't getting on; the marriage was no longer working (Adrienne came into the world in a family that was going to disappear). I'm an only child".–"Only child!"–"Yes; I had a brother, but he died of meningitis; when I was born, my parents no longer wanted me".

Silent reflections: what role did the loss of the first child play in the equilibrium of the couple? What repercussions did the mother's depression (loss of Adrienne's elder brother) have on the constitution of her immune system? Into what kind of atmosphere was the newborn female baby received? Did the parents' mental dispositions have a genetic and immune somatic impact at a time when the infant is not yet able to distinguish between psyche and soma, the most vulnerable period of life?

'A lady, a nursemaid, brought me up and I stayed with her until I was 23 years old. I went to school". She said this in a way that suggested her time at school had left no lasting impressions, the primary trauma had never been erased and her mother's absence was deeply inscribed in all her behaviour and thinking, but what was most remarkable was the dispassionate tone of her account, a detachment and remoteness.

"I got married when I was 23 years old; my husband was an engineer". Here again she did not retrieve any memories in connection with their meeting or the marriage; as in automatism, there were no associations of ideas, as if an entire part of her psyche had been erased. Then, suddenly returning to the present, she stated: "He found a girl 20 years younger than me; you know, he and I were the same age". The reference to this painful episode seemed to interrupt her mental functioning–there were acute anomalies in mental functioning–and she fell completely silent.

She stopped crying; I connected this silence with her reference to the abandonment and, to re-establish our contact, I mentioned the possibility of other relationships in order to break the isolated silence (both hers and mine!). I referred to the fact that there were people around her and reminded her that she might have at her side the affectionate and warm presence of human beings who loved her. I said this in order to restore our communication; to convey that after all she was no longer alone and isolated now; "and your friends?" I preferred to pursue the warm relational aspect than the line of enquiry into the trauma, which I thought incurred the risk of aggravating her condition.

"I've got some friends and I see them regularly ..." Suddenly, as if there was a further interruption of functioning, she looked at her right hand and arm; the body seemed to manifest itself in this long dialogue, to come back to us; the body manifested. "Thirty-one years ago I had a small circular tumour on my right wrist (JIM, 1996)[21] and there was no further mention of it ... I got married in 1946, I was 23 years old. (She mentioned her first cancer). People I knew teased me about this; they laughed, "oh, you've had your cancer!" I had a transplant that was successful".

I wondered what might have changed in her environment to explain the presence of a malignant tumour–a new trauma, a mourning or a severe life event–and, as our conversation had in some respects been highly elliptical, I concentrated on both her parents and her nursemaid, as they were the three main people mentioned besides her children; this was followed by a strange episode of temporal confusion, as I have indicated above.

"My mother was born in 1860 and my grandson was born in 1970; I think my mother died then (!); my father died when he was 60 years old of a heart attack in 1960 or 1965. My nursemaid died at the age of 92; I was all she had and I took care of her".

When she mentioned her nursemaid, some childhood memories surfaced. "I learnt the violin; I was the best-dressed girl in the district". She then lapsed into contented silence and narcissistic reverie about this happy time; everything was not dark, there had been a happy period in her childhood. I continued to pursue the investigation by asking her about her dream life. "In my dreams, I'm always in trouble; I never have nightmares; I never do very well but that doesn't frighten me; I didn't have the most beautiful dress or hat either". This contradicted what she had said slightly earlier but here an extremely impoverished dream expression was observable, like a present-day contraction of psychic functioning due to the illness or a developmental failure of symbolic expression relating back to deprivations and frustrations that had been difficult to overcome through thought; "that doesn't frighten me", she said, indicating her capacity to confront things. To explain this particular point, I returned to the image of the nursemaid and the psychiatrist who took over the affective role. "Yes, my psychiatrist is strong like my nursemaid" (the nursemaid's maternal body); she then interrupted this train of thought to state: "It was suggested that I study medicine, I was intelligent and was easily capable of studying ... My godmother, who was my mother's sister, would have done anything for me".

This revival in a narcissistic mode, as she put forward her intellectual abilities, seemed to me to be the consequence of our meeting. Conversation at the bedside of a severely ill patient in a hospital room is never easy; therefore, since I was afraid of tiring her despite knowing that this relationship might also benefit her, I thought I should end our discussion while taking extreme precautions. Adrienne perceived my thought about leaving her and, sensing that we were about to part, she returned to the subject of her solitude. "I rarely stay alone in my own company; I go outside to attend clubs, I don't like being on my own. If I go on holiday, I go to my holiday place and I have my grand-daughters to visit me there, I take care of the children" ...

"I'm not afraid", she seemed to be saying, "but I'm anxious when I'm alone in my own company". Once again, this thought took her back to the earliest days of her life and the traumatic experience that accompanied them. Our separation undoubtedly made her re-experience the many separations during her life.

I felt sad as I left her, wondering how good her chances of survival were and how I might be able to help her. This patient's distress was heart-rending and I left her room feeling intensely moved, because her destiny reminded me of some recent family mournings. However, what I sensed deep inside me, this mute anxiety connected with her references to recent mourning experiences, was also some questioning about my patient's life prognosis, experienced in the countertransference; the unavoidable outcome was confirmed to me a few minutes later by the doctor.

Commentary

There are several points in this observation worth consideration: a trauma that has endured from conception to birth, resulting in the abandonment of the child, whose survival was ensured by the nursemaid as maternal substitute. This parental violence was attenuated by the father's financial support and maintenance until this patient's marriage. This responsibility was then assumed by her husband, who thus took over from the nursemaid, but this man then threw the patient back into the terrifying universe of her earliest days of life: in his turn, he abandoned her in an intensely violent way (the day before their separation, she did not know that he was going to leave her). She then went through a six-year depression, interspersed with suicide attempts and a beneficial encounter: a psychiatrist with a maternal physique who ensured her survival just at the time when she was about to retire.[22] This final abandonment must have thrown our patient once again into a phase of essential depression, giving rise to a progressive disorganisation.

Let us reconsider each point of this investigation in turn and elucidate these in conceptual and clinical terms in order to understand their meanings.

Adrienne's final abandonment is experienced as the loss of an object, a mourning, with all its associated consequences. Freud states this explicitly: "Mourning impels the ego to give up the object by declaring the object to be dead and offering the ego the inducement of continuing to live" (1917, p. 257). In fact, a part of ourselves, the narcissistic part, is deeply tied to the object and it is this part that we are at risk of losing in mourning: "We are in danger of being dragged into death in turn by this part of ourselves that is connected with the object. The other drive aspect, namely our aggression, is also affected by mourning; although we have loved the object, we have also hated it and we have even wished for its death, so that there is a risk that this death wish signals our own fatal end, since the loved object forms part of us in the form of narcissism. Is pain therefore "like a signal that awakens us to life?"" (Amar, Couvreur & Hanus, 1994, p. 14).

In Adrienne's case, I shall consider the questions of narcissism, the object relationship, the expression of the suffering and, finally, the non-manifestation of the aggressive drives. The above-described schema of the progress of mourning does not seem to be fully applicable here. First, there seems to be no mental suffering, unless this pain is being masked by taking morphine, or again, as is frequently the case, the physical pain is replacing the mental pain caused by losing her affective relationship with the psychiatrist, as if the psychotherapeutic relationship over the previous twenty years had in some way been limited to the role of protective shield and maternal support.

There is no suffering, as she said: "I'm not suffering"–the hospital care seems to have made her regress to a period of happy calm. She is being taken care of (by the Mother Hospital), so why–she suggests–should she be suffering? However, this does not eliminate the trauma of abandonment, as the abundant tears and sobbing at the beginning of our conversation revealed. According to the anamnestic report, Adrienne has manifested no defensiveness or hostility throughout her life. The aggressive drives have never been expressible. She exists and dwells in the silent expression of suffering; her mother abandoned her, she got married, then her husband abandoned her and she has never fought to protect her interests; she is in deep distress.

On the basis of these reflections, I can take a different view of the psychoaffective problem and contemplate it not from the oedipal perspective, which constitutes a highly elaborated organisation of mental functioning, manifesting itself through imaginative richness, a wealth of associations of ideas and journeys between present and past that did not appear in the discussion, but in a different mode, as with the preceding observations; namely, *a deficiency in the organisation of the preconscious*. Adult preconscious functioning is largely based on the representational system established in early childhood; *these deficiencies are usually connected with an affective unavailability on the mother's part towards the young child*, either because she has gone through long periods of depression, or because her preoccupations have distanced her from the child. In either case, it has not been possible for a representational system connected with affects to develop fully and thus provide psychic functioning with its basic substance. It can thus be understood that such a deficiency in the organisation of the preconscious may form an obstacle to mental elaboration and, more specifically, to the work of mourning. The usual work of mourning is described as follows: "It consists in gradually sifting through the deceased person's qualities and failings (for the subject). Generally, the deceased's qualities are acquired, with an acknowledgement of his failings and then set aside. The taking into oneself (incorporation) of the deceased person's qualities constitutes both an enrichment for the subject and a testimony of gratitude towards the deceased (still present, at least, in the subject's unconscious)" (Marty, 1991, p. 35). The time period required for this work of mourning varies.

Now, once again, I do not see any sign of this work of mourning taking place in Adrienne; she has some confirmed deficiencies in the organisation of the preconscious; at no time has she talked at length about her mother, nor has she described or manifested any hostility–likewise for her nursemaid–which suggests to me deficiencies in the processes of projective and introjective identification. The only association of ideas to have been expressed, as I had asked for it, was the representation of the bodily identity of her psychiatrist and her nursemaid, both of whom had round figures. I wondered about her early infancy and the defect in the constitution of certain elementary psychic processes that are fundamental to the development of the psychic apparatus. This stage of thinking is inferred by Sigmund Freud in *Inhibitions, Symptoms and Anxiety* (1926): "Mourning occurs under the influence of reality-testing; for the latter function demands categorically from the bereaved person that he should separate himself from the object, since it no longer exists. Mourning is entrusted with the task of carrying out this retreat from the object in all those situations in which it was the recipient of a high degree of cathexis" (p. 172).

The question that arises here with Adrienne is whether her relationship to her mother, the object of early relations, has been constituted? Given that the object cathexis cannot be fulfilled in nostalgia, it is understandable that in the reproduction of situations in which the binding with the object has to be undone, this binding has not taken place according to the psychic processes usually described by psychoanalysts.

How can a binding that has not taken place be undone? Moreover, this situation creates anxious affects. Freud distinguished two types of anxiety in this respect: the child's anxiety about strangers and his anxiety about losing his mother, which are both painful to experience. "The very young infant cannot yet distinguish between temporary and long-term absence. The repetition of reassuring experiences then enables him to establish this distinction. When the mother is absent, he feels nostalgia without despair. If the need is not current, the mother's absence is only a worrying danger. If a need is felt, this absence becomes a traumatic situation" (Amar, Couvreur & Hanus, 1994, p. 31); this is the case here.

I shall therefore form the hypothesis of an early defect in the attachment to her mother in the early months of life. What is the connection between this deficiency in the establishment of early psychoaffective organisations and the fragility of the skin; why a melanoma? This is what I am next going to examine.

In *Beyond the Pleasure Principle* in 1920, Freud had indicated using the first topographical model that the Pcs-Cs system encompassed the other psychic systems. This system at the frontier of the external and the internal world thus has two aspects: an external and an internal aspect. This idea was taken up by Esther Bick (1968), who emphasised the need for introjection of the breast-mother, serving as a containing object, for the creation of the fantasmatic psychic capacity for internal and external spaces; this external object thereby enables the most archaic parts of the personality to be interconnected. "This introjected containing object is experienced as a skin. It functions as a psychic skin", states Didier Anzieu (1994, p. 72), who founded this basic concept. He explains to us that this skin-boundary function is the precondition for the onset of the processes of splitting and idealisation of self and object. Anzieu distinguishes two functions of this psychic skin: an external function that receives physico-chemical excitations from the external world–the protective shield, Freud's *Reizschutz*–and an internal function that perceives signs and enables traces to be inscribed, an envelope of communication or meaning. The protective shield is exclusively turned towards the exterior. The part turned towards the interior receives the full force of endogenous stimuli and drive excitations. The only possible functioning then is a psychic functioning; that is to say, giving meaning to the internal world, since the interlocking of the envelopes is constitutive of the psyche, the apparatus for thinking thoughts, containing affects and transforming the drive economy. The pathology of psychic envelopes provides an explanation that accords with the contributions of psychosomatic theory and treatment. For Anzieu, the continuity between the two surfaces of excitation and communication, depriving the human being of the fantasmatic capacity, gives rise to operative thinking (Marty), which is reflected in exchanges with others by communications in which emotional life and associative thinking are severely impoverished. Anzieu concurs with studies by psychosomatic clinicians when he states that: "In these cases we often find an early relationship with a mother or a maternal substitute that is characterised by indifference, whether this is due to a depression or conjugal problems with the father or ... connected with what Green terms the 'dead mother'" (1990, p. 31).

This maternal lack at birth is also revealed by some somatic symptoms that were recorded by the doctors in the department without actually having been linked with the symptomatology as a whole. These consisted in recurrent pneumopathies and a positive reaction to a tuberculosis test at the age of 30 years old and therefore the fragility of the respiratory membrane.

Spitz described these symptoms in his remarkable study of the first year of life (1965). Spitz distinguishes two types of affective lack that give rise to severe disorders: partial affective lack and total affective lack. The first type is the famous anaclitic depression; the second is the well-known phenomenon of hospitalism, accompanied by symptoms of severe deterioration that continues to worsen with irreversible consequences. Drawing inspiration from Spitz's research, I hypothesise that, as a result of being abandoned by her mother at birth, Adrienne has a partial affective lack since a maternal substitute took over in the months following her birth, but we do not actually know in what conditions this took place. The observation of a sample of 123 new-borns in an American institution studied by Spitz indicated behaviour in the form of *weepy retreat*, weight loss and insomnia, as well as *an increased propensity for complaints in the respiratory tracts*. This behavioural syndrome gradually worsens over time, but if the mother or a maternal substitute returns after three months of separation most children make a recovery; otherwise, a two-month transition period is instituted during which all the above-mentioned symptoms are consolidated. However, even if the mother returns, Spitz considers it unlikely that there is a complete cure; *he thinks that the disorder will leave traces that will emerge over the years*. This early deficiency in object relations blocks or at best hinders personality development. In this respect, I had been struck in my meeting with her by Adrienne's lack of aggression *and Spitz confirms that aggressive manifestations are conspicuously absent in children suffering from either anaclitic depression or hospitalism*. The mother's early absence deprives the child of protective shields and he is therefore unable to find any target for discharging his excitations; "he first becomes weepy, demanding and clings to everybody who approaches him ... after two months of uninterrupted separation, the first definite somatic symptoms appear" (1965, pp. 286–287).

The need for good object relations during the first year of life is now better understood; in the absence of these, psychoanalysts and psychosomaticians hypothesise that disorders that emerge during the constitution of object relations may become a serious handicap in the transition to adolescence and to adulthood. In her studies of children, Margaret Mahler (1952) suggested that there were two possible developments in psychic functioning here: an autistic development and a symbiotic development. On reaching adulthood, the first type of child "shows lack of contact, withdrawal and in extreme cases, catatonia. The symbiotic child, on the other hand, finds his counterpart in the adult who shows certain forms of pathological infatuation, extremes of dependency with strong suicidal tendencies" (Spitz, 1965, p. 295).

Adrienne's two suicide attempts after her husband's abandonment are in my view attributable to this fragility in the relationship with her mother, which could not develop satisfactorily although a nursemaid had replaced the absent mother. It can therefore be supposed that the aggressive drives that seemed to be absent because they were not manifesting were defused from the libidinal drives and were therefore turned back against the self, causing depression and illnesses. In an effort to counteract the aggressive drives, the libidinal drives turn towards the "self" in order to protect it and become exhausted in the efforts to secure the individual's survival.

The recent essential depression (with the end of the therapeutic support) reactivated this syndrome of abandonment by returning Adrienne to this long series of maternal severances, resulting in symptoms that initially puzzled the doctors. I would like to discuss the onset of anorexia; this current essential depression must have been preceded by some identical depressive phases following which Adrienne fell ill: a melanoma on her wrist (following the deaths of her nursemaid and her father) and then, in the years following the dramatic separation from her husband, psychic distress with a near-triumph of the death drive (two suicide attempts), depression in the classical sense of the term, recurrent pneumopathies and, I hypothesise, the beginning of the cancerogenesis.

I am basing this hypothesis partly on studies by cancerologists concerning the average duration of cell growth, given that the growth began slowly and then accelerated. By considering the growth rate, we can (Tubiana, 1994) determine the history of the tumour: first its emergence–that is, the time at which it started to grow, then subsequently the time at which it spread, giving rise to metastases. With a constant doubling period (exponential growth), Tubiana considers that "the tumour has grown for a time equal to 30 doubling periods, that is 90 months, when it reaches a detectable size. A hidden seven-to eight-year period has therefore preceded its clinical emergence". He then states that metastases "cannot be detected until several years after the primitive tumour has been destroyed" (1994, p. 71).

In this respect, Adrienne had conveyed to me, with a mischievous look and a shrug of her shoulders, that she thought her cancer was long-standing: "They (the doctors) believed that my current illness was caused by the separation from the psychiatrist!"

Why had she criticised the doctors? Was this a means of capturing me in a maternal kind of connection? Was there an emerging manifestation of aggression? I would never know.

The regression caused by the revival of the initial traumatic shock reveals not only the turning of her aggressive drives against Adrienne but also deficiencies in her identification and projection mechanisms. In fact, the inhibition of the projection mechanism makes it impossible to deflect aggression externally to protect oneself against it, which is reminiscent of a failure in what Klein calls "the life instinct in its internal struggle with the death instinct" (Riviere, 1952, p. 291). The gradual onset of the identificatory function has been disturbed by the mother's withdrawal at Adrienne's birth, combined with the difficulties of finding a nursemaid in her first few months of life. This functional fragility has been reactivated during the various traumatic episodes of her life, leading Adrienne at an unconscious level to what Paula Heimann calls "the despair that there is nowhere anything good ... Phantasies of this kind create a vicious circle; the inner situation gets worse, because it cannot be relieved by introjecting a good object, but the worse it gets, the more introjection becomes inhibited. *It is a state of mounting anxiety and distress*" (Riviere, 1952, p. 158; my italics).

The regression recently induced by the trauma of abandonment (by the psychiatrist) is affecting the secondary processes, since the concept of time is gradually disappearing. The mental confusion, probably revealing the attack on certain nerve centres by metastases, is accompanied (deficiencies in the central nervous system) by a temporal regression to unconscious primary processes, a phenomenon with which we are extremely familiar in psychosomatics from many clinical observations. The confusion initially applies to the date of her first melanoma and the deaths of her father and nursemaid as well as to her mother's age: the first confusion concerns the birth dates of her mother and her nursemaid, as well as their dates of disappearance. First Adrienne confused her nursemaid's and her mother's lifespans, which is understandable since she had never seen her mother again; however, she attributed an astounding longevity to her mother since according to my calculations her mother would have been 110 years old and therefore 53 years old when Adrienne was born, which in fact corresponded to her nursemaid's age, her biological mother's image having gradually disappeared over time. Her nursemaid and her father died in the same year, deaths that preceded her melanoma by one year, which was minute in size at the time it was discovered.

If we consider the biological growth periods of the tumours and consequently the latency period of unobserved silent growth, we must then take account of the anxiety generated by the probable disappearance of her father, suffering from cardiac disorders and of the nursemaid, with declining health, of whom Adrienne took care. She had been living with the two people who really mattered to her.

The silent growth phase of the first melanoma would correspond to the phase preceding the deaths of the two people whom Adrienne most loved. This temporal confusion at the time of my investigation made her regress into a world from which time had been eliminated, bringing her closer to the deceased whom she had never mourned.

Further commentary: the transition from the psychic to the somatic

There is one final point to consider before we proceed to an analysis of the psychosomatic interrelations. I would like to discuss Adrienne's discourse, with its strikingly impersonal references to people and her apparent lack of emotions in relation to life events; I must affirm, however, that some emotions were expressed at certain moments in the investigation; namely, in her tears and particularly in this deeply distressed expression. We know nothing about the people mentioned: the forenames of her nursemaid, children or grandson; her every word was spoken without any tonal variation in the delivery, without any quavering in her voice, without any manifestation of what she was feeling ... The only evidence of any emotions at all was in her reference to her ten-year-old grandson, when she cried and then quickly stopped. This is a behaviour often described in psychosomatic investigations; somatic manifestations unconnected with associative chains and without any evocative power. She had cried at the beginning of the session and the close relationship she had formed with her grandson may point to incidents that are likely to have occurred when she was his age. It is through the factual account and the lack of emotions that I might be able to introduce the possible communication with the somatic: what role is played by the interrelation of the nervous system and the immune system in Adrienne's case?

I know from experience how difficult it is to assess the psycho-affective state of a patient who is taking heavy doses of morphine, but Adrienne talked about herself to me as if it were about someone else (dissociation process possibly resulting from neuronal disorders). The situation did not develop during the interview, as if throughout this contact the only psychic changes produced related to my internal disposition. These symptoms of essential depression revealed the reduced level of libidinal tonus and the presence of an operative life, combined with the above-mentioned erasure of the crucial psychic functions–identification, projection, association of ideas–and, above all, hyposymbolisation (disappearance of the dream and fantasy life).

This essential depression must have been established several months earlier, after the psychiatrist left to retire, as a prelude to the progressive disorganisation, thereby leaving the death instinct as "master of the house" (Marty, 1966). Here I confirm the intuition of my doctor colleagues; they were correct on this point.

Adrienne showed some emotion when she mentioned the separation and abandonment by her husband, then remained rather cold and distant throughout the rest of our discussion, as if this were a rare surfacing of emotion. *It significantly revealed the traumatic loss of her first object–the mother–and the incapacity of her psychic apparatus to bind the overabundance of excitations from this initial trauma, which was in fact reactivated by my questions.* In the practice of psychosomatic investigation, the traumatic risks and therefore the dangers of aggravating the somatic illness can be alleviated by the investigator's empathy.

The lack of emotional manifestation relates back to the distinction between affect, emotion and feeling: I therefore reiterate that affect is an internal state with biological and psychological aspects, emotions are the biological dimension of affect and, finally, that feelings are the psychological aspect of affect, mainly expressed through the imaginary and through associative thoughts (Pédinielli, 1992). The exclusive presence of emotions in Adrienne would thus underline the predominance of physiological manifestations (tears) and behavioural responses. These observations concur with those of well-known clinicians such as Dr Eugene Pendergrass, President of the American Cancer Society, who in a lecture in 1959 stated: "Anyone with an extensive experience in the treatment of cancer is aware that there are great differences among patients" (1961, p. 891) in terms of growth rates and recovery, giving an example in which "The sequence of events ... strongly suggested a relationship between the emotional stress and the reactivation of the disease ... a long-standing, intense emotional stress may exert a profoundly stimulating effect on the growth rate of an established cancer" (pp. 892–894).

In the 1960s and 1970s some hypotheses concerning stress and immune responses led to confirmation that high levels of emotional stress increase vulnerability to diseases. Constant stress gradually weakens the immune system and increases the vulnerability to illnesses, especially to cancer. Emotional stress, which has effects on the immune system, also gives rise to hormonal imbalances. These can increase the production of abnormal cells precisely when the body is least capable of destroying them.

From the beginning of the 1980s, immunologists (such as Ader, Ghanta and Solomon) conducted some research that sought to build a bridge between mind and body (Rossi, 1993) by seeking to demonstrate how behavioural conditioning can either inhibit or alternatively stimulate and increase the responses of the immune system. They proposed that:

1. "Apparently all of these tissues and cell types are in communication with each other as well as with the central nervous system and the autonomic and endocrine systems through a variety of messenger molecules that have been given many general names such as *immunotransmitters, cytokines, lymphokines, interferons and interleukins*, as well as more specific designations such as *interleukin 1 or 2 (IL-1, IL-2), interferon gamma and tumor necrosis factor*" (1993, p. 218).

2. "Many of these immune components [immunoglobins, cytotoxic T-cells, suppressor T-cells etc.] are open to psychosocial influences ... Acquired immunity thus has a specific developmental history in each individual; its functions are therefore particularly subject to the influence of state-bound information acquired in early life experience" (p. 223).

3. T- and B- lymphocytes operate with their receptors, which "are like locks that can be opened to turn on the activities of each cell ... the keys that open these locks are the messenger molecules of the mind-body: the *neurotransmitters* of the autonomic nervous system, the *hormones* of the endocrine system and the *immunotransmitters* of the immune system" (p. 223).

It is clear from observation that the mind regulates the large systems in a complex interrelation, but research has not yet ascertained how this functioning works in detail; it involves hypotheses and a conviction based on an accumulation of data concerning neuroanatomical and neurochemical evidence. In short, immunologists suppose that *the immune system is capable of communicating with the hypothalamus and the autonomic and endocrine systems via the intermediary of immunotransmitters* (Hall et al., 1985).[23] This research by immunologists has provided the basis for formulating highly sophisticated hypotheses concerning oncogenesis and, more particularly, the relations between psyche and soma. The majority of individuals do not develop cancer, although cancer cells are constantly produced, which suggests that the body has a system of immune surveillance that seeks out and destroys cancer cells before they can develop into detectable tumours.

Stein Keller & Schleifer (1985) have demonstrated that *a slight depression in the system of immune surveillance* is enough to increase the individual's sensitivity to pathogenic agents, particularly those that are constantly present and threaten bodily integrity such as cancer cells. These findings have led to a theory of oncogenesis, namely that *"tumor formation takes place when those components of the immune surveillance system are depressed or underactive"* (Rossi, 1993, p. 241; my italics). According to this research, cancer is to be considered as a communicative disorder at the cellular-genetic level. It seems that there are only two basic processes that can lead to these communication errors, regardless of the cancer type, namely *the creation of oncogenes and the malfunctioning of tumour-suppressor genes*. With a view to developing psychophysical therapies, Rossi puts forward an explanatory model of psychophysical relations, based on all the hypotheses of cellular biology put forward above. I think that such a bold statement is admirable but premature, as there is a risk of raising hopes–particularly in patients suffering from autoimmune diseases–that a psychotherapist cannot fulfil at present; there has yet to be a serious epidemiological study on the beneficial effects of psychotherapies.

This model concurs with our preceding observations on Damasio's somatic markers, namely: *the encoding of information that is supposed to transcribe our emotions, behaviours, fantasies and thoughts at the cellular level*. The stress model seems highly apposite, since corticosteroid hormones, administered at a high dosage, can cause a reduction in the number of T lymphocytes within a few days, which would facilitate the emergence of the pathologies that they normally control.

The hypothesis that I would put forward here is that the trauma of abandonment at a crucial period in the development of the immune system has weakened Adrienne at both a somatic and a psychic level. There has been a failure in the establishment of a primary somatopsychic organisation at an archaic stage in which only primary processes predominate. The connection that is made between emotion (due to the trauma of the abandonment), behaviour and the weakened immune system specifically determines the relations between the central nervous system (mainly the hypothalamus) and the immune system. This somatopsychic registration defines the modes of functioning and establishment of behavioural relations. "Somatic compliance" occurs at the hypothalamic-hypophysary strategic level; psychosexual development has been severely impeded, leading to a structure of *behavioural neurosis*. This is characterised by the emergence of rapid malfunctionings confronted with a quantity of major excitations and, according to the proposed model, their transmission to the first somatopsychic organisation. We are then faced with fluctuations that increase in magnitude until a maximum point beyond which there is an explosion–emergence of the first cancer thirty years later–then a return to a laminar state brought about by the family presence. A new cycle then begins when she is destabilised by her husband's departure, then quickly stabilised by the substitutive psychotherapeutic care. Finally, this time interval of random length is interrupted by a turbulent period accompanied by rapid depression of the immune system according to the above-described processes. An irreversible process of progressive disorganisation has been irreversibly implemented.

This path towards chaos[24] (new state of psychic and somatic equilibrium) leading to death can be amplified by a contribution from Joyce McDougall (1989), who postulates the existence of an archaic sexuality with sadistic and fusional aspects as the possible source of psychosomatic regressions, which can be considered as defences against mortal experiences.

This would suggest that because of her rejection at birth by her mother, who had not in fact mourned her first child, Adrienne has attempted throughout her life to preserve a fusional unity with her mother. Archaic hysteria, a concept defined by McDougall, strives to preserve the body in its entirety and the subject's life; this concept refers to the child's preverbal mode of thinking and his somatic expression. The distress and inner anxiety experienced by Adrienne's mother caused the initial fundamental violence, so that Adrienne had to endeavour throughout her life to maintain a fusional relationship with maternal substitutes in order to remain alive. There was no anxiety and no alarm signal, which meant that the sources of anxiety were not symbolisable; they were subject neither to repression nor denial, nor disavowal but to the mechanism of repudiation (foreclosure) which, confronted with psychic pain, expels the affects outside the psyche. This initial trauma prevented the constitution of a strong ego through the various above-mentioned processes, namely: incorporation, introjection and identification. Adrienne's oedipal organisation was based on an archaic initial organisation from which the paternal image was partly absent, so that she was confronted with the boundless void of the maternal inner space with its frightening and mortal aspects. Moreover, the repetition mechanism, securing survival, ultimately led Adrienne to create a somatic object–the melanoma–in order to be able to live in the illusion of maternal fusion. Rage and fear of abandonment had led Adrienne down a path of mortal despair.

Adrienne puts me in mind of Fritz Zorn's unfortunate hero, another cancer sufferer, who stated: "My father is dead; my mother is still alive. In a certain sense, my mother has killed me; but I don't want to hate her and cannot hate her for this because I know that she doesn't know she did it" (1982, p. 181).

Sanjay, AIDS or "an imaginary illness!"

From psychosomatics to somatapsychics: "You've got six months left at most", the impersonal doctor told Sanjay.

"The moment we discovered what we were bearing inside us, like the stone of a fruit, the shock was so immense, so strong and so explosive, that our bodies felt too frail and too narrow to support it"; this is how Maxime Montel (1994) in his book *Un mal imaginaire* [An imaginary illness] confronts us with something intolerable–the announcement of the illness that will lead a person to the end of his days. This news has a traumatic effect, with enormous psychic repercussions; on receiving this news, the patient is almost siderated if he has not been psychologically prepared. This is the eternity of the moment, in which time seems to have frozen: "This moment was beyond everything. It defines all the others that follow; I constantly have to turn back to it; I'm still there, I've stayed there, in this upsurge of terror" (p. 50).

Some readers may be surprised that I am presenting a case of acquired immune deficiency syndrome (AIDS) when doctors state that hospitals are growing empty and that there is a prospect of AIDS becoming a curable disease. I shall present a patient suffering from this illness as well as some better-known diseases; my purpose here is to show that regardless of the illness, it is the whole clinical picture including somatopsychic and psychosomatic functioning that has to be taken into consideration. How does this process take place for an AIDS patient?

Let us start with a brief return to some recent developments. As the latest Congress in Washington showed, although triple-drug therapy fails to improve the condition of 15–20% of patients, it is a different matter for patients recently infected with the AIDS virus: infection in every case of less than three months. The triple-drug therapies conducted for example at the Aaron Diamonds Center in New York have produced some highly encouraging results, with the virus remaining undetectable in blood tests. However, some organs act as reservoir sanctuaries in which the virus remains hidden while waiting to reactivate. "Although the virus is undetectable, this does not mean that it has been eradicated", as Dr Ho from this centre stated; the difficulty is how to know when it is safe to conclude that the virus has permanently disappeared and above all after what time-span it will become possible to decide to stop the medication at risk of witnessing a resurgence of the virus load.

We should remember that although patients from developed Western countries are benefiting from current triple-drug therapies, this is not the case for all the populations affected. Statistics published by the World Health Organisation reveal that around 17 million people were infected with the human immunodeficiency virus (HIV) at the end of 1995; the majority of cases–11 million–were in sub-Saharan Africa, followed by Southern and South-East Asia with 3 million, Latin America with 1.5 million, North America with 750,000 and Europe with 500,000. HIV-AIDS infection began to spread in the early 1980s among homosexuals and intravenous drug-users in some urban districts of America and Western Europe, as well as in men and women with multiple partners in some regions of the Caribbean, Central and Eastern Africa (Pillonel, 1996).

Let us now return to Sanjay: Sanjay[25] is from Guyana; his grandparents lived in Madras in Southern India. In 1498, the coast of Guyana, in north-eastern South America, was sighted by Christopher Columbus; the native population are American Indians (Warraus, Arawaks, Caribs, Wapishanas, Arecunas etc.), who represent only 4.5% of the total population; the largest ethnic group (over 40%) are descendants of the Indian emigrants from whom Sanjay originated. He was the youngest of a family with eight children; his parents spoke Hindi or Tamil at home but he had never learnt his mother tongue. It seems that his parents, as is often the case for emigrants, used their language of origin to communicate without being understood by their children. Sanjay was 41 years old; he was an elegant man who took great care with his appearance. He was very tidily dressed and well-presented; his beard and hair were always carefully trimmed. Through an administrative error, he had a different surname from his parents, which had prevented him from emigrating to the United States with his mother when he was 29 years old. The mother left with all the other children and he remained alone with his father, who was a sub-officer in the fire service. A few years later, his father had been accused of misappropriation and he too then emigrated to the United States, but in secret. Sanjay was left alone and he still thought that he could survive his parents' departures and that his destiny was to prosper in his own country. He thought he had not been treated equally to his brothers and sisters; his father had favoured his elder brother and had forced Sanjay to work when he was seventeen years old in order to pay for his food and lodging. This situation of differential treatment by the father made him hostile towards his elder brother, who was financially supported by the family. However, this hostility was never expressed, as the unhappy episode of his desire to marry revealed; after his two-year military service, he met a young woman whom he wanted to marry and introduced her to his parents, who opposed his marriage. Sanjay complied and then bitterly regretted doing so. He talked very little about his childhood but told me that he only began to walk very late (at around two years old) and also to speak. He had carried out many different kinds of work, mainly as a hotel manager, repairing and making zinc roofs, but he had never made very much money and his financial position had never improved. I think that his situation as the youngest child and the extremely close-set births of his brothers and sisters drove him to become a seducer, as the only strategy for obtaining attention from his mother. Sanjay saw himself as a seducer, a "womaniser". When he talked about women, his face was overshadowed by regret and bitterness; later, in his therapy, he warned his young therapist in a farewell message by telling him, "don't follow the girls too much". Sanjay had probably contracted HIV from sexual relations with a prostitute from Surinam during one of his trips intended to make ends meet at the end of the month.

He found it difficult to talk about his fourteen-year-old daughter, who lived in the same town as him, but since his departure he had heard nothing more from his daughter or his wife; this part of his life was as if secret, being unknown to his parents, who had forbidden him to marry.

Sanjay felt his illness was a punishment from God; this was the Christian God since, for unclear reasons, his parents had baptised him in the Seventh-Day Adventist church, which is well-known for its proselytism; it was as if they had sealed his fate by this act. Sanjay appeared to have had nothing more in common with them: he had a different surname, different beliefs and–later on–a different country!

Sanjay left Guyana for Holland; one year later he arrived in Paris, where his health suddenly deteriorated; he was suffering from headaches and an increasingly dry cough that he seemed to be ignoring. One morning, feeling feverish, he took himself to a hospital accident and emergency department, where he was told that he was suffering from AIDS. He thought that the illness would disappear after treatment with antibiotics. He knew nothing about this disease. For six months, Sanjay was in hospital and he received intensive medical treatment; he had developed pneumocystosis and the advance of cerebral toxoplasmosis had left him with difficulties in walking. He also complained of impaired vision. His psychotherapist thought that the illness had affected his memory, concentration and verbal expression.

From a medical viewpoint, he was classified as C3, which indicates an advanced stage of the illness.[26] The illness had hit Sanjay with full force, leaving him with difficulties in walking that meant he would use a crutch. HIV has a marked neurotropism and it is very quick to penetrate the central nervous system, resulting in cognitive, behavioural and motor changes, mnemic disorders, impaired concentration, a slowdown in mental processes and so on (Moulinier, 1996). However, I shall take up some medical observations that may have an impact on the patient's awareness and subjectivity; in this respect, the HIV-related encephalopathy was not accompanied by an obnubilated consciousness, which applied until an advanced stage of the illness. Confronted with his cancer, Freud communicated to us his state of mind: 'I can't get used to the idea of an existence on sufferance" (letter concerning his cancer to Lou Andreas-Salomé, May 13, 1924, quoted by Jones, 1957, p. 475).

The different stages of the illness

When the Association took care of Sanjay, providing him with a flat, some financial assistance and therapeutic support, he had just come to the end of six months in hospital; he had no financial resources, work or social insurance and was visiting France as a tourist. He had become an entirely different person; suffering at the deepest level inside and completely exhausted by six months of intensive treatment, he seemed to be in a state of post-traumatic stress and nervous exhaustion that resembled burn-out, the intense stress syndrome. He was thrown into this state following the terrible news, which he initially denied, thinking that it could be treated with antibiotics; this state was accompanied by partial amnesia–he was unable to remember the events surrounding his hospitalisation. We should bear in mind here that the doctors had given him little hope, restricting his life expectancy to six months, thus plunging him into the abyss of imminent death.

The hypothesis I shall advance here is that the surplus of mental excitations quickly flooded Sanjay's defences, given his weak psychic structure, precipitating him into an essential depression, paving the way to a progressive disorganisation with a life-threatening prognosis. The essential depression exacerbated the depression in the patient's immune system; we remember the close-set births of children whose mother later abandoned Sanjay.

Early on in their meetings, his therapist rightly indicated the patient's difficulties getting to sleep and hyperactivity, which meant that during the first few therapy sessions his patient would stand up and walk around in a highly agitated state.

After he left hospital, Sanjay's hope was restored and it was almost with enthusiasm that he arrived at the Association's head office to begin a supportive psychotherapy, which he experienced in a different way from the usual therapeutic relationship. For him, his therapist was an Association member and as such would occupy the position of the Mother who abandoned him in transferential and fantasmatic terms. He planned to return imminently to his work selling goods on the metro. During the early sessions, he presented a behaviour dominated by internal excitations that he managed to reduce by getting up, waving his arms around and talking like an auctioneer; he was shouting rather than speaking. This behaviour might well surprise a Western therapist but it was difficult to interpret because the patient came from a culture in which bodily movements and expressive gestures are favoured modes of communication; also speech volume can be higher than in Europeans, apart from inhabitants of Southern Europe, who express themselves using a loud voice accompanied by physical gestures and movements. I should mention here the difficulties in interpreting infra-verbal behaviours and signs, which can be misleading. However, we must accept the hyperactivity, the factual discourse, the amnesia and the lack of complaints about psychic or bodily suffering as signs of an operative life into which he had been precipitated by the illness. A smile would often cross Sanjay's face and an apparent joviality seemed to conflict with the general picture. These seemed likely to be manifestations of the child's joy at rediscovering a good mother, whom he greeted in this way.

This raises the problem of how to assess emotional reactions in a patient from a foreign culture, who was totally isolated from his family environment and lacked either financial resources or any means of communicating with the hospital staff whose language he did not speak. As he lay bedridden, Sanjay's psychic apparatus had to make recourse to the mechanism of foreclosure or massive rejection of affects connected with his precarious situation in order to survive. Here we are faced with the phenomenon, described in detail by McDougall, of patients with this capacity to expel affect-charged experiences outside the psyche. She explains: "Analytic observation of these alexithymic and operatory reactions to psychological stress enabled me to see that *these were frequently defensive measures against inexpressible pain and fears of a psychotic nature*" (1989, p. 25).

Thus, in parallel with the advance of the illness as it developed in the body, I observed a process of essential depression and progressive disorganisation that might be aggravating the somatic disorders. Accordingly, we could see biological processes at work destroying the immune system as it was overtaken by psychic processes propelled by the death drive as it gradually returned towards instinct in an increasingly regressive mode. I should like to discuss this gradual disappearance of mental life as it returned towards the soma.

Somatic malfunctionings are factors that instigate psychic disorders with repercussions on the soma according to a model that corresponds to those used in economics,[27] namely a cyclical model which, instead of producing regular cycles following a sinusoidal curve, leads to a cycle with an explosive magnitude until the system completely disintegrates. Here I am referring to the destiny of the psychic energy, which is surpassed in magnitude by somatic energy, bringing a progressive destabilisation in the homeostasis of the somatic functions that leads to death. In the Appendix, I shall present the preliminary outline of a mathematical model, taking up the various hypotheses to which I have referred during the presentation of the clinical observations. If this is how it is in theoretical terms, what is the clinical reality? Is it possible to stop or decelerate the processes described? I think this can be done using a combination of medical and psychotherapeutic treatment.

The doctors had given Sanjay six months to live, whereas in fact he left us eighteen months later: how can we account for this discrepancy? The medication certainly contributed to this survival, although in this particular case it was not taken very regularly or in sufficient quantities. We have to take into consideration the combined effects of the medication, the psychotherapy and the social and economic support from the Association. It is these three elements that permitted this survival, as well as the progressive mourning for life.

It is my view that this man would not have survived as long as he did without his therapist's help; in fact, the support provided corresponded with a resurgence of life instincts that had almost disappeared. The countertransference attitudes went through different phases: from anxiety to aggression aroused by the patient's fears of death, then from patience to admiration for a man facing a terminal illness and, finally, to the deep desire for human authenticity in order to give "a high-quality attentive listening" in a situation that was felt to be a tragedy. In addition to this, there was the role his therapist played on the "magical" level, which he was unable to appreciate himself; I want to discuss the unconscious role of the traditional healer at Sanjay's side to protect him from the malevolent virus.

The therapy sessions took place according to a ritual that could be decoded; for example, Sanjay talked at length about the medication while unfolding a prescription and asked me to read him some instructions, then went on to talk about how difficult some of it was to take. This ritualisation, common to many somatic patients, who use a proportion of their sessions to talk about their illness in terms of the medication, suggested to me the creation of an intermediate space that needed developing in order to facilitate the subsequent emergence of psychological problems, as if a transitional object were being created that was intended to become the substitute for the maternal protective shield; in short, a favourable space in which the psyche could manifest itself. Once the secure space is established, the session can be instituted. This is in fact what happened since once this ritual had been established, Sanjay talked about his mother's visit to Paris with his youngest sister. "She came to Paris to have a holiday, without bringing me anything–a few dollars, something to buy myself a little radio with–she advised me to stay in hospital".

His mother had come and abandoned him again; he then neither expressed resentment nor seemed to feel any distress. He mentioned a daydream that might reveal to us his emotional experience: "There is a man sinking in the sea and despite all his efforts to get back to the surface, he fails to cling on to the rocks jutting out from the reefs and he sinks into the abyss, almost inexorably". This return of the trauma in the form of reverie is a sign that mental work has resumed as a result of the psychotherapy and it reveals the deep distress he was caused by his mother's abandonment, which relates back to all the other abandonments; he cannot cling to the rocks, the maternal body–he will sink and disappear.

In the same session and in many that followed, Sanjay showed his attachment to the Association-good mother figure and wondered what would have become of him without it. The Association did not abandon him: It provided him with food and accommodation, some pocket money and a therapist. The Association had become his new Mother.

His relationship with the Association was characterised by an ambivalence that he had not expressed in his relationship with his mother; namely, his fears of being abandoned once again; he did not want to disappoint the people who were helping him. Any remaining aggression was therefore projected on to his elder brother, who had been able to benefit from their mother's support. At the end of sessions, he would present gifts that were intended fantasmatically to maintain his relationship with the Association-Mother, to perpetuate this bond. These modest gifts are, as we know, highly ritualised in many Eastern and Far Eastern countries and they are designed to establish and consolidate affective and social relations.

Sanjay was afraid of asking too much from the Association and then being rejected by it because of his demands, which he judged to be excessive. This situation was experienced in a maternal mode by his therapist. He felt like a bad mother who was not acceding to the child's demands, increasing his dependence and resentment by therapeutic means.

Moreover, the patient put his therapist to a severe test because of the emotional burden that was not formulated by Sanjay but was present in the relationship. The unconscious anxieties he thus transferred related to the attack on the body and organic functions that manifested in many everyday difficulties and, as the dream indicated, the constant, silent presence of death.

This presence of death manifested itself in Sanjay's return to God; he attended mass every week; he felt guilty for having led a sinner's life, like the prodigal son. In the same way, he had left his father and squandered his "health" capital during his travels; now, he wanted to return to his father who had preferred his elder brother to him. Intuitively, he mentioned his lateness to walk and talk, to which he attributed his father's and mother's rejection of him; the choice of religion had permanently severed him from his cultural

and parental roots. They had not inscribed him in their system of fil-
iation; he had in my view become a "prodigal son", *despite himself.*
Had he been a wanted child?

We know that fragility in a human being is established at an
early age and the same process is found at work here as well; under-
stimulated by the family environment, not recognised as a member,
he had no place in the exchanges or any possibility of speech, which
explained his delayed motricity. We understand the various aspects
of this patient's emotional life: He could not express his aggression
towards his mother, who had returned to the United States; he had
never really expressed it. As a result of his therapy, there was a
resumption of his mental life, restoring some of his hope and an
improvement in the sensations of internal comfort. This enabled him
to turn back to his father in order to discharge his bitterness and to
return to his childhood and adolescent past; then, as the path of
return to his father seemed to be closed, since the latter had chosen
his other son, he chose the spiritual path to discharge his affects that
were beginning to manifest themselves. "There is the side of hope
and there is the dark side", he said, "this hidden side that may be the
world of shadows". He then explained that the Bible says that a man
lives for three score years and ten, asking in that case how much
time he had left to live, as he was 41 years old? After a silent pause,
the therapist replied to him: "No one knows when his time will
come"–this question always reminds the therapist of his own relationship to death.

As a result of the psychotherapeutic endeavours, Sanjay put on
some weight and made efforts to improve his nutrition, as if a period of calm had been instituted. A space for life opened up, which
gave the patient some respite. There is now a better understanding
of the hope that triple-drug therapies can give to patients who have
recently contracted the virus. His impaired mobility (neuronal problems are the most frequent, in nearly 70% of patients) meant that sessions could no longer take place at the Association's head office; his
therapist went to see him in the therapy rooms. Sanjay gradually
regained a degree of autonomy and returned to his recent past and
the discovery that he was HIV-positive. He struggled to re-cathect
his body, shattered by the illness: "I'm still fighting ..."

These moments of respite suddenly gave way to another phase
of the illness; he was struck down by an epileptic fit along with the

scar of a lesion from the toxoplasmosis and he had to undergo a new stage; he went back into hospital. His therapist continued to see him in this setting. This stage of the therapy was difficult for the patient and his therapist on many levels. From one fit to the next, Sanjay lost more and more of his autonomy and he felt he was on the threshold of his final journey. His therapist understood his distress and experienced this episode in terms of helplessness and the futility of the support provided. I think that this presence was fundamental although very emotionally gruelling for the therapist, because Sanjay continued to maintain the internal equilibrium of life impulses despite the somatic disorganisation. This is the deep sense that we have in these psychosomatic therapies; the therapist is on the side of life—he fights.

Having returned to the therapy rooms, Sanjay made some practical arrangements with the help of a care assistant; he seemed to be sinking into a depression that was the penultimate stage of the events that accompany the end of life (Kübler-Ross, 1995).[28]

He wanted to compose letters to his father and his mother and then abandoned this idea. He did not want to write to his daughter and refused to consider making contact with her, thereby perpetuating in his turn the abandonment to which he had been subjected! Sanjay thought about the end of his life and wanted to be buried in a coffin; he wished to follow the precepts of the Church and distanced himself from the Hindu practices of cremating the body; he did not believe in their concept of reincarnation. He was experiencing a kind of internal struggle between obsessive thoughts about his parents and his desire to forget them; but how can anyone forget their parents?!

His physical condition was steady and he benefited from an advanced form of treatment. He lived in the moment and took his medication at highly irregular intervals; the decision to institute pain-relief medication was taken by the medical staff without informing the patient. This is a sensitive problem to mention but every change in treatment must be clearly stated to the patient while taking every possible precaution to alleviate the emotional impact; it is important that there should be a genuine therapeutic team that takes decisions together. Faced with the silence of the medical team, the psychotherapist took on the burdensome task of confirming to his patient that this was palliative care that presaged the end. This new change of direction and its emotional overload resulted in the therapist experiencing some temporary backache, as he faced his patient's death alone. This should make us give more serious consideration to the need for multidisciplinary health teams to deal with these situations.

The therapeutic conversations continued and it was evident that life was gradually ebbing away from the narcissistic core that constitutes the person (at which the self-preservative and sexual drives converge); Sanjay squeezed his therapist's hand and spoke of "a door that has not yet opened; this is the door that is opened by God".

Ten days later, Sanjay died; his father and his brother came to attend his funeral. They were present after his death.

Studies concerning the efficacy of psychotherapy are only just emerging; in Sanjay's case, I can attest that his psychotherapist enabled him to live eighteen months beyond the timescale accorded to him by the first doctor.

CHAPTER FIVE

The psychotherapy of
somatic patients—the case of Nina,
a woman from the Maghreb

A t her last therapy session, Nina, a young Jewish woman
from the Maghreb, looked me straight in the eye and said:
"You know, I think I'm pretty now; for all these years you've
been like a father to me". She then turned her back on me and
walked away quickly and happily. Nina had been referred to me by
a colleague nearly nine years earlier for some psychosomatic psychotherapy (Stora, 1996), which was necessitated by her illness,
acute systemic lupus erythematosus. I had not thought that this
therapeutic undertaking would last this long, nor had I known that
it would take me down paths leading back to my childhood and
adolescence and to the traditional healing practices of the Maghreb.

In this chapter, I shall address the problems raised by the psychotherapy of somatic patients; the observations I have presented in
this work have often featured patients from cultures beyond Europe.
It seemed to me more appropriate to present a case example that is
often found in hospitals and health centres, namely patients from the
second generation of people who have immigrated to France. This
will enable me to discuss both the technical and the theoretical problems posed by somatic patients, as well as to address the cultural
dimension that is an essential part of the psychotherapeutic process.

Nina was born in France, having crossed the Mediterranean in her mother's womb. She was suffering from an autoimmune disease: acute systemic lupus erythematosus. The recognition of self and non-self is a basic function of the immune system; this recognition is a process established during ontogenesis. During foetal or neonatal life, the developing immune system learns to recognise the self, defined as the individual's complete set of molecular structures. The immune system is confronted with these structures in the environment of early life. How then does an organism lose the capacity for self-recognition? In 1953, Brent, Billingham and Medawar conducted some experiments (Fougereau, 1995, p. 20) that began to reveal the workings of an essential immunological process known as immune tolerance. Through some experiments on allogenic transplants, they demonstrated how one living organism (B, for example) can develop a tolerance towards the cells of another living organism. Subsequent research studies have modified hypotheses concerning immune tolerance by positing the existence of a process in which reactivity to the constituents of the self is lost. This would account for the way in which the loss of specific receptors of the self can cause long-term damage to the organism. This impairment in the faculties for distinguishing between self and non-self gives rise to a formidable array of autoimmune diseases, such as myasthenia gravis, multiple sclerosis, juvenile insulin-dependent diabetes, autoimmune thyroids, acute systemic lupus erythematosus, rheumatoid arthritis, autoimmune haemolytic anaemia and scleroderma. In autoimmune diseases, the organism's immune system behaves like an aggressor towards its own constituents. These autoimmune diseases account for a high morbidity rate in France, with several million people suffering from them. These are chronic illnesses that develop over many years.

In recent years, I have observed around fifteen patients with acute systemic lupus erythematosus; during the anamnesis, all these patients had reported similar circumstances surrounding their mothers' pregnancies: family, social or political troubles, or being unwanted as a child. I have not yet been able to explore this avenue of research but I should like to introduce the hypothesis of neonatal and/or postnatal fragility in the immune system of people who suffer from autoimmune diseases in later life. What might have been

the consequences of unsettled pregnancies for the processes of identification of self and non-self?

One patient stated: "Doctors claim that lupus is not one of the so-
called psychosomatic illnesses, but autoimmune diseases are a form
of self-destruction. Producing antibodies against your own organism strikes me as absurd. It seems to me that there must be some
kind of psychological disturbance at work. Several friends of mine
have advised me to consult a psychotherapist".

After these brief preliminary observations about immunology,
let us move on to my patient's therapeutic progress. Several questions arise when we are dealing with French-born patients who have
grown up in a family environment that belongs to another culture.

To begin with the standard question as to the role of the illness in
the psychic economy: what role was this illness playing in Nina's
mental functioning? As a psychotherapist, what role was I playing
in the transference and countertransference and what role was my
patient getting me to play in assisting her cure, caught between the
different dimensions of her ancestral religion, her "healer" grand-
mothers and the terrifying invisible world of the "djinns" with
which they seemed to be familiar? We should remember that this
patient grew up in a Judaeo-Arab environment. A psychoanalyst has
a responsibility to know about his patient's cultural environment.

In the course of this account, I shall be describing the various
stages of the treatment, set in the context of Jewish North African
history and strange beliefs that I have also held myself since earliest
childhood–beliefs that gradually resurfaced in the transference and
countertransference relationship.

My colleague had referred this patient to me because she
thought that I would be able to give her better care than other therapists because she came from the same region of Algeria as I
did–the province of Constantine. Once again, without my having
asked for this, I was having a "foreigner" referred to me; this situation reminded me of the course of my psychoanalytic career that
began in 1973 and the long series of patients I had treated, almost
all of whom were immigrant foreigners either living or staying in
France. Consciously or unconsciously, my colleagues only remembered me for my identity as a French Jew of Algerian origin, send-
ing me patients from Vietnam, Brazil, Canada, Martinique, India,

China, Japan, Morocco ... and, of course, Algeria. Having grown up at the confluence of three cultures–Jewish, Berber-Arab and French, this cultural awareness of various peoples has been useful to me in my therapeutic practice but it has never before formed the subject of a clinical or theoretical study. Psychoanalytic training in the psychoanalytic societies of the International Psychoanalytical Association creates an institutional superego in order to obtain from analysts a standard form of behaviour that ensures a quality and a guarantee of psychotherapeutic and psychoanalytic treatment; this training can then act as an impediment to treating patients who do not fit the standard setting. Having encountered some difficulties in listening to my patients and treating them, I kept asking myself questions about the specific nature of their mental functioning and of the transference–and especially the countertransference–relationship. I am referring here to the unconscious interrelations between the multiple components of my identity and those of patients.I wondered how to interpret the words, silences, emotions, behaviours, thoughts and somatic disorders and who it was that these patients were addressing. Was it their apparent perception of me as a Parisian French psychoanalyst to whom they had been referred, or was it other aspects of my identity perceived within the unconscious—unconscious relationship? A look, a smile, a hand gesture, a particular style of greeting, a specific intonation–all this non-verbal communication that imbues the relationship between patient and psychoanalyst–might be important factors here.

Beyond these words, silences, emotions, behaviours and somatic disorders, were there imaginative dimensions and unconscious (oedipal and pre-oedipal) fantasies that were inaccessible to me?

Another question then arose: in the treatment, was I dealing with individuals whose identity had been constituted in exactly the same way as Europeans or with members of familial and/or tribal communities whose identity (in the western sense) had never been constituted? If the latter were the case, this raised a serious problem of psychoanalytic technique, since the technique developed by Sigmund Freud is primarily aimed at individuals. In fact, what was the right way to deal with these patients who talked about themselves using the first person plural? I am referring to the distinction emphasised by anthropologists to differentiate between cultures: the individualism/collectivism dimension (Hofstede, 1982-83).

As a foreigner among foreigners, a foreigner among members of my "native"[29] country, I was living with this "suitcase syndrome" described by Tobie Nathan (1994). I had to take a dual approach here: to restore my own connections with a specific past that had been partly or totally repressed and never analysed and to re-learn from my patient how the imagination was constituted in Jews from my native town and its region in order to help her to find her own way.

The specific identity of patients necessitates some anthropological and historical digressions in my account. The analysis of French patients in an environmental and historical context that is familiar to both analyst and patient does not involve considering elements of the frame of reference known to both participants; it is a different matter with foreign patients.

My research was assisted in two ways by my acquaintance with Tobie Nathan; at our first meeting, I attended an ethnopsychiatric consultation in which the audio system was located in a circular space occupied by around 20 fellow therapists who were sensitive to various cultures to which they belonged. I did not immediately understand the lever effect exerted by what Tobie Nathan terms *a therapeutic operator* in creating the therapeutic psychic space necessary for establishing a transference relationship and connecting the cultural, sensorimotor and psychic worlds. This session tested me and seemed somehow to respond to my needs in terms of transforming the therapeutic relationship with regard to my patient. The second occasion, an administrative meeting, reserved a final surprise for me when in some parting words Tobie Nathan encouraged me to be myself with my patient, directing me towards a genuine interpretation that lifted the prohibitions of the western psychoanalytic superego. I was encouraged to travel the multicultural worlds of my origins without feeling guilty. As well as this support from Tobie Nathan, I also had some encouragement from Pierre Marty, who was familiar with my therapeutic treatment and who enjoined me to make my own way in an unknown universe.

Let us first set the patient, her family and her therapist in their geographical and historical context. Although I am referring to a place that I know well since I was born there, this is a story that could have taken place in any region of the Maghreb.

Back to origins: the geographical and historical setting

The ancient city of Constantine, named after the Emperor Constantine, was once the capital of Numidia and known as Cirta. At the period when Nina's family left, this city had 145,000 inhabitants, including nearly 100,000 Muslims; its 40,000 French citizens included a Jewish population estimated at approximately 20,000. This high figure lent a particular character to this austere city, which for every monotheistic religion symbolised the second most important city of reference; accordingly, the Jews of Constantine called it "little Jerusalem", with good reason, since the way of life was deeply puritanical and Muslims, Jews and Christians were all fundamentalists about 50 years ahead of their time!

Without going into much further detail about the history of this city, I would observe–drawing on the theory of the influence of climate on the character traits and behaviours of various peoples put forward by the great philosopher Ibn Khaldun (1332–1406)[30]–that the geographical location, the continental climate and the large number of mosques, madrasahs and Koranic schools helped to reinforce the strictness of religious observance. The city of Constantine was built on a rocky peninsula at the northernmost point of the High Plateaus at an altitude of about 600 metres. This imposing rock appears set apart from the surrounding plain by a wide canyon with sheer cliffs of 200 metres in depth. Along the base of this canyon meanders the Rhumel river. This watercourse supplied by the Bou-Merzoug approaches the city from the south and flows under the Devil's bridge, a strange place at the foot of the gorges, a source of inspiration and terrifying beliefs; it then runs beyond this bridge and close to some hot springs that have given rise to some healing practices to which we will later be returning. The Rhumel then flows into a large ravine. Having reached the northernmost point, at which the Kasbah was built, it forms a series of cascades and moves away from the city towards the North. As the Rhumel crosses the city, at the foot of the gorges and the El-Kantara bridge, its waters surge momentarily under a high roof, re-emerging and disappearing several times; at places where the river disappears, some impressive natural bridges have formed that are 50 to 100 metres wide. Some hills rising over Constantine suggest an image of the city that Muslims say resembles a vast burnoose of which the Kasbah forms the hood. It has also been named *Belad el Haoua*, the ethereal city; the city of the ravine and the city of passions, *haoua* meaning air, ravine and passions.

Growing up in such an austere city is a strange experience, since it inspires a sense of proximity to God but also to the dark side of mysterious forces hidden in the depths of the abyss. Religion has exerted a strong influence on this city throughout its history. In the 16th century, Constantine was a centre of the Enlightenment, like Bejaïa under the Beni Hammad and Tlemcen under the Marinids. Such a deeply religious atmosphere can only exist in a city whose inhabitants adhere to a specific set of practices.

The district known as Ech-Chara had been allocated by Salah Bey to the Jewish inhabitants of Constantine. This extended from Place Négrier to the Boulevard de l'Est, on a north-west/ south-west axis and the left bank of the Rhumel ran along one side of the district. The 1889 guidebook does not give the number of synagogues but as I remember they existed in numbers proportionally equal to the number of mosques in relation to the number of inhabitants. I shall conclude this brief description of the city with a reference to the hydrotherapy centre at Sidi-Msid, which exerted a particular fascination for the Jewish and Berber-Arab populations because of the traditional healing practices. It is reached by a lift that makes a vertiginous descent into the gorges of the Rhumel and the Sidi-Msid springs are then 400 metres away. There are four springs of sulphurous water, which emerges from the caves to form some natural bathing-pools. The third bathing-pool hollowed out by the Romans is known as Bourma-er-Rabat. Every Wednesday, Jewish and Muslim women go there and, according to an ancient guidebook, perform their devotions by throwing in tomina–cakes made of honey and semolina–while burning incense there, as well as by ritually slaughtering poultry.

These traditional practices shared by the Jewish, Berber and Arab peoples do not emanate from the influence of Islam, as has often previously been incorrectly stated; it is necessary to go further back in history to study these customs and practices (Chouraqui, 1972).

Nina's anamnesis and diagnosis

"Psychoanalysis mistakes characteristics that are exclusive to contemporary western societies for universal traits of human nature" (Bergeret, 1993, p. 828).

The colleague who had referred Nina to me had provided me with a brief report summarising the key elements of the consultation. She was described as a darkly dressed, good-looking young woman, with large rings under her eyes and a slightly tragic expression. Nina had been referred by a general practitioner who diagnosed what he called "psychosomatic" manifestations, such as dizzy spells, diarrhoea, tremors and agoraphobia, as well as allergies to many medicines. This doctor stated that the lupus erythematosus from which Nina had been suffering for twelve to thirteen years seemed to have stabilised, but that her recent mourning for her brother, who had died in tragic circumstances, was making her unable to tolerate the disease any longer and, furthermore, that she was having "panic attacks". Following her brother's death, the patient had just come out of hospital after two days for an operation on her right index finger after a staphylococcis infection caused by local injections of hydrocortisone. In Nina's mind there was a very clear connection between her finger and her brother's death. She concealed her deformed finger and I finally found an interpretation of this in the traditional therapies; she had broken off a platonic but important relationship with a man to avoid revealing this deformed finger. Nina was the last-born in a family of five children–two boys and three girls. Her elder brother had also suffered from dizzy spells for ten years but had "lived with it", whereas she refused to accept them. Three years earlier, her father had died of a heart attack and her brother's recent death had increased her distress. During this investigation, she had been asked about her dreams: Nina dreamed about white and pink, saying "which, for us, is not good". In accordance with the psychosomatic theory of mentalisation, the doctor inferred from this an impoverished imagination, commenting: "No image behind these colours". I had a different interpretation: as with many other peoples, dreams are interpreted predictively (Freud, 1912-1913): white and pink, like every other colour, therefore have very different cultural meanings from one people to another. Later I was able to observe that these colours were associated with the oedipal connection with her deceased brother and with the castrating punishment resulting from her operation (deformed finger); hence, this apparently mysterious remark that this was "not good". This observation raises a problem with the above-mentioned concept of mentalisation, for it is difficult for a western observer who is not very familiar with certain cultures to assess the symbolic capacities of a patient who is foreign to his culture.

Nina stated that she had been stifled by her mother and her brother. She described the life of "a Jewish tribe of North African origin". She was the one who looked after her mother and she stayed alone with her all day; she felt so lonely that she would call her neighbour, who would then call the doctors, sometimes three times a day. What role was played by the repetition of this daily appeal to the doctors? Why did she address this to her neighbour? This neighbour was called Ghalia; she was from the Maghreb & Nina saw her as a terribly attractive woman, indeed as a sorceress who might have been responsible for her illness! A sister of Lilith! At the end of the interview, the doctor had an acute sense that "the cultural and family burden" was weighing heavily on this young woman. The cultural difference during this discussion became apparent from some trifling remarks that went unnoticed by a European doctor, which is understandable given the anthropological distance between them. I am gradually going to reintroduce some historical elements that will enable us to decipher these emergences of a composite identity. I shall embark on a first digression on the subject of Lilith; I referred to seduction when I mentioned this mythical figure in relation to Nina's neighbour. Lilith plays an important role in the imagination of more than a thousand million of the earth's inhabitants. Who is she? What place does she occupy in the psyche of this part of humanity? Which figures in western mythology are similar to Lilith?

Mythological digression: Lilith

In this account, I shall refer to some traditional rites of initiation and protection that are associated with Lilith's invisible presence during labour and birth. In Nina's case history, her birth and her mother's pregnancy had in fact occurred in difficult and mysterious circumstances. During both pregnancy and labour, the lives of both mother and child were perpetually threatened by the djinns (high infant mortality as well as high maternal mortality during and after labour). To drive away evil spirits (djinns) and protect his family, the future father has to perform many protective rites: at the beginning of labour, the woman has to untie her hair, which is thought to open the natural orifices for the expulsion of the new-born baby. The father writes many talismans known as *shemirot* to summon protection from God and the guardian angels. Most of these talismans make explicit reference to *Lilith*.

Accordingly, at the time of the birth he draws three circles on the walls of his wife's bedroom, in which he writes: "Adam, Ava, chutz Lilith"–Adam and Eve, protect us from Lilith. The character of Lilith is particularly fascinating; in the Bible she is referred to only by Isaiah, but she appears in many books of the Talmud[31] and in the Zohar.[32] She is often considered to be Adam's first wife, before God created Eve to console Adam for Lilith's departure. What was the reason for this departure? According to Talmudic tradition, Adam's first wife Lilith quarrelled with him, ostensibly about their way of lovemaking; this argument concealed the couple's male/female rivalry as to which of them would have supremacy. Lilith contested Adam's claims to be the head of the family and, faced with his attitude, she invoked the Ineffable name. This invocation is supposed to summon God's power of aid (but who knows the Ineffable name nowadays?) and at this invocation, Lilith grew some wings and flew out of the Garden of Eden. In despair, Adam turned back to the Almighty who, moved by his distress, sent three angels to search for Lilith, but in vain. This is how Eve came to be created from Adam, thus being close to the man. I shall return to the contrast between two female figures surrounding Adam. Lilith is a long-haired female demon with wings. She roams the world by night, assuming dozens of different names; she visits women in childbirth and strangles their newborn children. She also attacks human semen: it is said that at night, the man who directs his desire towards Lilith will suffer misfortune. Lilith induces men to have sexual relations outside marriage and also tries to oust the legitimate wife. In the Zohar, Lilith, this winged female monster, appears as a prostitute, a damned soul, a faithless lover and a liar and she is also black; this colour relates to the identification of Lilith with the Queen of Sheba, who according to Jewish and Arab traditions was in fact a djinn, half-human and half-demon. This fascination exercised by Lilith over men and these mysteries is reminiscent of the Sphinx, who as we recall is a female monster; moreover, one of Lilith's names that appears in a 14th-century shemot is *Striga*, also known as the Strix or Sphinx. This association comes as no surprise because historians trace Lilith's origins back to Babylonian and even to Sumerian mythology: it is said that two demons, one male and the other female, called Lilu & Lilitu, may be etymologically related to the Hebrew word *laylah* (night). A Hebrew inscription asking the Almighty for protection from Lilith appears on a Syrian stele dating from the 8th century B.C. This fear of Lilith intruding on the thoughts of a couple during sexual relations is the source of an incantation in the Zohar that urges a man to direct his thoughts to the holiness of the Lord during the time when he is joined with his wife. This ritual act is a reminder that Lilith's true home is in the depths of the sea, for the seductress is likened to the *Sirens*. Lilith shares the marine realm with many sisters, or is she in fact their mother? The Greek Nereids with their fish tails; the female bird sirens; the Hydra, the many-headed sea snake, daughter of Echidna and sister of the Sphinx are all monstrous creatures that bear monstrous children; they are the great seductresses whose sexual act ends in devourment.

These phallic-bodied women (the sirens' tails) have a pregenital sexuality; they represent oral devouring impulses, anal impulses of object-mastery and narcissistic tendencies in their relationships. They can only transmit their drives to their children in an archaic functioning according to the model developed by Melanie Klein. "A woman who is unable to renounce her phallic power becomes a sterile and destructive envious person. However, the man also has to see this phallus-woman over whom he wanted absolute mastery fly away (just like Adam with Lilith) and she henceforth threatens his sex, his power and his children" (Duparc, 1986, p. 701). To accede to genital sexuality, that is to the prototype of Eve's sexuality, every woman has to renounce the power of pregenital sexuality, the witch's anal archaic power. The predominance of symbolic mythological aspects that constitute the patient's preconscious gives us an indication of how to proceed in pursuing associative chains in the psychotherapeutic treatment: both on the traditional ancestral level and on the western cultural level.

In summary, by paying homage to Lilith, the mother of tailed demons, witches align themselves firmly on the dark side of life and its archaic stages, for psychoanalysts the pregenital dimension. Accordingly, Lilith represents the first stage in female psychosexual development.

Continuation of the commentary

Using the psychosomatic classification to establish a diagnosis in the light of the symptoms we have ascertained, this might initially be formulated as follows:

Neurosis with uncertain mentalisation (doubt) accompanied by diffuse anxieties (periods of distress), hypochondriac, hysterical and apparently masochistic symptoms, with deficient integration of passive satisfactions. States of suffering without desires or any modification at the onset of the illness, which does not become an object of cathexis; latent depression; inhibition; avoidance or suppression of representations; suppression of drive expressions in behaviour; acute anomalies in mental functioning; cultural or religious tradition weighing on psychosomatic functioning. Acute or subacute depression (symptomatic in the psychoanalytic sense); recent unresolved mourning; recent restrictions–accidental or otherwise–of physical activities; relative (at least provisional) reorganisation in a hypochondriac mode. This final observation refers to Nina's compulsive behaviour in calling the doctors on a daily basis to treat "fleeting" symptoms that nevertheless undoubtedly have a dual role and a dual interpretation.

A problem arises in using this kind of model with patients from non-western cultures; in fact, as I suggested above in quoting from Bergeret, western characteristics are not universal; the lived experience (state of suffering, depression, hysteria, hypochondria) is *altogether different*. We enter another universe; the western ethnocentric diagnosis has to incorporate another component.

This is what happened with Nina. I began her treatment from the perspective of a "western" psychoanalyst-psychosomatician and I had in front of me a young "western" woman, with each of us playing a role. However, I left every session feeling dissatisfied. In general (to give only a brief description) somatic patients reveal an impoverished mental life, few if any dreams, relatively inaccessible childhood memories, discourse that is deeply rooted in factual and current material, along with poor linguistic resources and, finally, a partial or complete inability to envisage the future.

What is the situation with somatic patients from other cultures? What interpretation should be given when patients have a non-western mother tongue? What happens when the illness has a different

meaning? We are confronted with a standard problem that is familiar to linguists: limited resources in the adoptive language and
abundant resources in the mother tongue, at least in terms of references and associations.

Nina did not fit this description. Was the neurosis with uncertain mentalisation perceived by a western doctor in fact based on a
weakness in the constitution of the preconscious? The expression of
some doubt during the diagnosis suggested that the doctor, who
was very sensitive to some non-verbal cues, had left the possibility
open for the therapist to modify the preliminary diagnosis, which
may in fact be revised in the first six months of the psychotherapy.
In my view, this was not the appropriate structure; this patient gave
me an uneasy feeling and revived some of my childhood memories
of traditional practices that Europeans describe as "magic", which I
did not dare to talk about with my colleagues (fear of contempt for
departing from the scientific behaviour of a rational western man).
What role might "magic" be playing in Nina's psychic functioning?
Was this way of framing the question not once again the result of
the ethnocentric influence of my cultural and intellectual conditioning? There were many facts, behaviours, emotional expressions,
memories and concerns that did not fit the customary "French" setting; the illness and the patient seemed to me to require a different
approach.

Nina went to the graveyard every Friday with her brother; she
called several doctors every day (but was it really to treat her?); she
turned to traditional rituals to treat her illness by calling on the serv-
ices of her grandmother and great-grandmother, both of whom were
"healers" and those of her neighbour living in the flat below; she
dreamed of buying luxury clothes and items, which she also found
to be a source of satisfaction. She wanted the doctor to "make her
fingers like before"; she did not think she was suffering from lupus
erythematosus! All this information was yielded only sparingly after
several years of treatment. This long series of findings required a
re-examination of the diagnosis concerning Nina's psychic functioning by setting this in her cultural frame of reference, which gradually resurfaced in my memory over the course of the treatment. This
is how, during the final years of her treatment, my therapeutic attitude developed considerably as a result of the analysis of my countertransference.

My research work is particularly focused on the psychopathology of the children of migrants; this involves an investigation into the psychic functioning of children from the second generation and the "repercussions" of the traditional family culture in the constitution of psychosexual development.

Nina's treatment proceeded in the most standard form of psychoanalytic psychosomatic therapeutic setting. This involved weekly face-to-face sessions, with a therapeutic attitude based on empathetic and warm listening that seeks to reduce the level of anxiety and therefore of excitations and, in certain cases, to revive the life instincts. After one year of treatment, the elaborative work of mourning for her father seemed to be proceeding well; the fear of death had diminished and a reorganising-reviving impulse was manifesting itself more strongly. Nina gained in confidence and she began to walk more briskly; she no longer had the look of an elderly woman dragging herself along. She smiled and spent three months making marriage plans; she also wanted to work. There were clear signs of a libidinal resumption. Over this year, Nina would summon doctors (emergency doctors, specialist doctors, cardiologists, hospital visits from the rheumatology department and so on) "whenever she felt unwell". This resulted in a continual procession that was undoubtedly expensive for social security. My interpretation of this intensely anxious demand was that in her struggle against the excitations connected with mourning her father (object loss) and the development of her lupic disease (attack on the bodily self) Nina had no other recourse than to use the medical staff as *protective shields* in a traditional healing mode, because of her deficient protective shields and anomalies in mental functioning.

My argument is that she was appealing to the doctors not to treat her but to protect her through their instruments and specific modes of operation (electrocardiograms etc.) from her unconscious fears and anxieties; she was thereby originally and inventively adapting the mode of treatment used by traditional healers.

The transference relationship was not yet sufficiently developed to substitute for these many demands and to provide a better-balanced life—that is to say, a satisfactory homeostasis—from one session to the next. Nina's frequent recourse to the doctors and, as only later emerged, to traditional healers delayed the transference impulse while protecting her from this connection. She did not yet have enough trust in me. At the end of the first year of therapy, I thought it would be appropriate to modify the classification of the mental structure thought to be inalterable with age, as well as certain characteristics of psychic functioning. The extent of the transition to behaviours seemed to me to indicate a behavioural neurosis; I think it was my western side that proposed this diagnosis, while another part of my ego was more inclined towards the diagnosis of a well-mentalised neurosis. Both aspects emerged in the interpretive mode: moreover, behaviours are well known to play a role in excitational discharge. Was it possible that the psychosomatic classification did not apply in this case? *What was the right way to approach a patient who referred to herself in the first person plural?* It was obvious that I was facing a problem for which I bore some responsibility; in fact, on more than one occasion I had the feeling that Nina was not alone in this hospital room where she came to see me. Her family was present as she said "we" or "one" but never "I". Psychoanalysis can only treat individuals; how can we treat people who belong to a human group that constitutes the first reference of identity? Was my psychotherapeutic treatment not going to separate Nina from her family group, her tribe and deprive her of her favourite defence mechanisms?

Here I am indicating a technical problem concerning the progress of individual development: would too much individuality distance Nina from her family and set her at odds with traditional values? What was the right way to proceed? I made what seemed the most appropriate choice by pursuing a middle course–strengthening the ego without depriving her of the traditional frame of reference–but I may have been mistaken ...

After one year, Nina reduced her daily dose of cortisone and dreamed of platonic love relationships in the image of her relationship with her brothers. As the last-born in her family, she settled into satisfactory affectionate relations with them in an infantile regressive mode. The progress of the sessions stalled: she was saying very little. I then got her to talk about herself, her family, what she enjoyed in life, her professional experiences, her schooling and, above all, what came to her mind in our conversations, what she was feeling and her memories. All this was gradually established, but she did not understand the necessity for this treatment; the 45-minute sessions were severely truncated; after half an hour or often less, she would look at me and say: "There, I've nothing more to tell you" and her feet would begin to move quickly, as if a mental excitation were turning into an impulse to "flee" and cut short the session. What was she repeating in this way? Was it her relations with her father, or her brothers? Whereas with French patients, it is easy to adopt the parental perspective and play masculine and feminine roles, in this treatment I was clearly identified as a man and I think that in the transference she identified me with her brothers rather than her father. The important role played by the eldest brother in North African culture is well known; this is particularly the case when the age gap with the father results in the brother or brothers standing in for the father figure. Her father's death, followed two years later by the tragic death of René, the brother whom she loved most, occupied most of the sessions during the first five years of treatment. Following these mournings, Nina had consulted a doctor who had referred her to our hospital; her illness had worsened in the meantime.

Nina made a pilgrimage to the graveyard every Friday for several years to visit her father's and her brother's tombs. Her elder brother accompanied her and gradually a form of brother/sister couple was constituted. The cult of the dead, mentioned above, continued in Nina's flat, since René's bedroom had become "taboo". It was occupied by René's shadow and, in this modest flat, the mother and the two younger sisters of the family lived in the same room. Nina shared her mother's bed and her other sister had a small bed. Her brother's clothes were carefully preserved and had not been given to other family members or to the poor according to Jewish custom. Nina admitted that this was not really in keeping with religious practices but stronger forces seemed to be at work.

A different process seemed to take place with her father: Nina still had the image of him as a generous man who gave so much money to the poor that he had nothing left for himself, as a man who took her by the hand on her birthday so that they could go to the bakery and buy a cake. This was a remarkable memory. There was a similarity between the mournings for her father and for her brother in the quest for the causes of death that propels us into the North African universe. In her father's case, Nina thought that it was the firemen from the emergency medical service who were responsible.

After her father's heart attack, first-aid workers from the emergency medical service had arrived and practised some cardiac massage; Nina stated that the first-aid worker had crushed his chest and that this had caused his death. The father had died shortly after being admitted to hospital. Her father was a force of nature; how could he have died? She did not articulate this, but it went without saying that the father had been the victim of a "spell!" Mourning gives way to the elaboration of hostile feelings towards the deceased; in Nina's case, these were projected on to outsiders (firemen, doctors, etc.) and family members. This search for the person or persons responsible for the death continued with Nina's murdered brother because his murderers had not been found. With this event, the quest continued on two levels: both in reality and in fantasy.

For several years, Nina and her elder brother turned detective. They had sworn on their brother's tomb to avenge him. They were searching for René's murderers but they both knew who lay behind it because they were making a distinction between the perpetrator and the person responsible. In fact, they suspected a cousin who was spending several years in prison, the son of one of the father's sisters. They voiced their accusations in more or less veiled terms and the family became angry. However, they challenged the person responsible: this was the grandmother, the father's mother. She was a rich and powerful woman but more importantly she was a "witch", someone who could cast spells, who cured women of infertility and who had used her powers (subsequently to cure her, as I discovered in the course of the therapy). Nina hated, admired and loved this diminutive woman whose husband was a tall, quiet and retiring figure. Everything was this woman's fault; over ten years after Algeria gained independence, she had called her children over, promising to give them a good start in life if they came to join her in Paris, which this family then did. While she was still in her mother's womb (three months), Nina's entire family moved to settle in Paris. They travelled by boat.

How were the development of the foetus and the genesis of the autoimmune disease from which Nina was suffering influenced by this journey and by her mother's depression?

This trauma of the suitcase and the emigration, combined with the adaptation to a different civilisation, inflicted some deep wounds on Nina's family. Every room in the grandmother's flat was used as living quarters by one of her children and his or her family. Nina's family lived in the kitchen (as we know, djinns particularly like to frequent places where water is found!) and her mother found herself in the daughter-in-law situation that exists in all Eastern and Far Eastern civilisations, namely to serve the family. It was she who washed the floor of the flat and carried out the lowliest household chores. Nina often talked about this, sympathising with her mother and contrasting their fate as a poor family with the paternal grandmother's wealth.

The elaboration of the mournings for her father and her brother occupied nearly four years of psychotherapy, accompanied by behavioural expressions on the part of Nina and her elder brother. The brother-sister couple would visit the graveyard every Friday and at Yom Tov (religious festival days); they carried out an investigation to find their brother's murderers.

All these activities had a dual therapeutic effect: managing the aggressive drives through projection on to the grandmother figure and a part of the family supposed to be responsible for the murder combined with reinforcing the narcissistic libido, resulting in the purchase of luxury clothes that restored her adolescent self-image and established a relationship with her brother René, who "draped her in fur coats and jewels". These clothing purchases were Nina's sole source of satisfaction in life.

In parallel with this therapeutic work carried out on the psychoanalytic psychosomatic level, *some traditional therapy was taking place without my knowledge. I had always intuited this because Nina's associative capacities seemed to halt from time to time and she would take flight by putting an end to the sessions. The rich abundance of traditional beliefs did not emerge in our sessions.*

It was only by analysing my countertransference, and therefore my own history, that I was able to find a way out of this therapeutic impasse. Despite being hidden from the patient's view, the psychoanalyst's personal history functions unknown to the patient in the context of the countertransference. At the intersection of several cultures, parts of which had been repressed, I witnessed a gradual resurgence during my therapeutic work of elements from my past that had not been mentioned during my psychoanalysis. These elements existed at the preconscious-conscious threshold, kept at bay by the force of repression. These elements had manifested themselves in the therapeutic setting as early as 1991 without my having been able to interpret the countertransference at that time; when I presented this case to a group of psychotherapists, I felt a strong urge to speak briefly about my memories of encounters with the spirits and my memories of attending traditional healing ceremonies.

As a small child, I had been terrified by the Shawia[33] tale of the existence of the djinns and their maleficent acts. At nightfall and whenever I went into a room with some water (kitchens, bathrooms, toilets, etc.) I would say some ritual words to protect myself. At night, in this small village in Aurès, my family's place of origin, I would be afraid of encountering someone when I travelled around because I did not know whether I was about to meet a creature from this world or from the other world and, above all, how to recognise it? We can of course laugh at the fearful imaginings of a very young child, but what are we to say when such a perception is an everyday experience for adults?! This familiarity with the djinns enabled me to understand intuitively that, in parallel with the medical treatment, it was also possible to make recourse to "magic" practices. As an older child, I had attended a strange exorcism ceremony for my grandfather, who was suffering from a severe illness that led to his death. Some Bo-Sa'adiya, descendants of African slaves who practise rites that are known in North Africa, had arrived with their drums and their strange clothes to chase away these evil spirits that were inhabiting my grandfather; this healing ceremony was called *salha*, meaning relief or reconciliation. I admired these men whom I had known as a small child and I was very afraid of them, because I was threatened with being taken away by them if I was not obedient. I also felt ashamed about their presence because I knew that these practices were condemned by Judaism but, in order to save a life, wasn't it necessary to try everything?

How much influence did my fascination with these practices have in determining my healing vocation? I always said that, failing being a doctor, what mattered the most for me was to care for my patients in the secret hope of healing them! It went without saying that I would never be a traditional healer but I think I owe them a great deal, as well as a debt of gratitude to my mother, who admired her brothers and cousins who were doctors and pharmacists but also sometimes called on healers, as we will see later. This personal account has been necessary for the remainder of my discussion, which consists in a methodological enquiry into the treatment of migrant patients at the intersection of several cultures. We must use several interpretive models: both on the psychoanalytic level and in terms of traditional healing methods.

As Freud states in *Totem and Taboo*, the dead are "powerful rulers" (1912–1913, p. 51). The ambivalence of human affectivity following the death of someone very close manifests itself in the externalisation of hostile feelings towards the dead person (unconscious desire to cause death) on to the deceased. "The survivor thus denies that he has ever harboured any hostile feelings against the dead loved one; the soul of the dead harbours them instead and seeks to put them into action during the whole period of mourning" (p. 61). These feelings are externalised by projection; however, in Nina's case, the problem was displaced from the dead on to the living: it was certain living individuals who had caused these deaths. It was therefore the witch grandmother who served as a projective screen for Nina's hostility for several years, but the progress of the work of mourning gradually modified this perception and the concomitant accusations. After four years of treatment, Nina began to dream and she brought me the following dream.

The fertility cave dream: in a dark cave, there is a woman in traditional dress; her face is almost indiscernible; she is swathed in light. For the first time we see Nina's grandmother in her life-giving role: she gives fertility to infertile women; also, Nina's elder sister had had a child through the action of the grandmother, this woman described as bathed in light. The Kabyle Berbers call this knowledge *l'eellem tilawin*; that is, knowledge that enables women to struggle against both infertility and death. The life-giving woman has the power to fight death. This capacity of the witch-healer is associated with her wealth; this woman therefore possesses an anal phallus, unlike Nina, who is the very image of castration with her deformed hand. The cave of hot springs also symbolises the maternal abdomen containing children and Nina later went on to describe a hidden room in her grandmother's flat that contained treasures that dazzled her child's wondering eyes: a real treasure cave! This helped to explain what it was that Nina envied about her grandmother: the phallus that she lacked. She had thereby displaced the hostility towards her father and her brother on to the witch. This hostility, arising from the repression of incestuous wishes towards the brother and the father, was characterised by the punishment of a castration that I would not go so far as to describe as symbolic but it is an interesting fact that the right hand should be afflicted, given the significance of the so-called hand of Fatima! This refers to an amulet, often worn around the neck, also called *khemsa* (five) in reference to the number of fingers on the hand and it gives protection from *"Aïn Ha-Ra"*, the evil eye. The word *yad* in Hebrew and Arabic means both hand and power. The name "hand of Fatima" refers to the Prophet's daughter; it represents the hand of God that protects, hinders or destroys. The right hand or hand of blessings is often distinguished from the left hand, the hand of curses. The hand gives protection, warding off malevolent acts perpetrated at its encounter and, in particular, the djinns.

It is related that one day when Mohammed's disciples were complaining about the prohibition of images, the Prophet soaked the ends of his fingers in some ink and, pressing them on to a sheet of paper, simply presented them with this in response. This figure represents the five perceptible forms of matter, or the perceptible universe as a whole. Why have I enlarged on this symbolic approach? In a treatment of this kind, symbolic thought is constantly present but never expressed. At this point in my account, I shall put forward the hypothesis of identical mental representations throughout a people that grows up in the same cultural environment, which therefore constitutes the reference-point for communication between the individuals who compose it. It is only the affective experience concerning these symbols that differs because this relates to each person's history and that of his family or tribe. Unlike Europeans, the preconscious in North Africa contains a highly structured set of shared references that are introjected to the ego ideal through parental identification. If a therapist is unaware of this system, he will be unable to establish a satisfactory transference relationship; the therapist will have the vague sense that something is eluding him. Now let us return to Nina's deformed hand; this is her right hand and specifically her right-hand index finger (the wedding-ring finger) and its deformity was connected in the anamnesis with her brother's death. It should be observed that these two events took place in very quick succession, with the deformity of her finger closely following the brother's death. Insofar as I have referred to symbolic meaning, it is because at this period in the therapy Nina rejected any reference of this kind and I attributed this associative void to the lack of mentalisation; I clearly needed to consider the therapeutic relational situation. This was not, I would stress, a case of conversion hysteria, but a somatic patient suffering from acute systemic lupus erythematosus. It is now time to embark on a second anthropological digression.

Traditional healing methods

I shall examine only the preventive traditional healing methods that form reference-points throughout women's lives, since I am discussing the case of a North African woman. Nina had grown up among women who followed these practices and during her childhood and adolescence her great-grandmother, grandmother, mother and all the women in their circle contributed to initiating her into the ancient way of being a Jewish woman in the Maghreb.

Happiness is always a dangerously precarious state for people who live in North Africa; our existence is threatened by these evil spirits known as *djinns* in Arabic or *mazikim shedim* in Hebrew. From a very early age, we are brought up in fear of them; they form part of our lives. These creatures have the ability to see without being seen, to change form and to move from one place to another in the flash of an eye; they are in the habit of eating bones and they are distinguished by their slit-like mouths. They run wild at nightfall and every new or unknown ill is imputed either to them or to the evil eye. I shall describe various rituals that give protection from these creatures but if you are afraid of encountering them, especially at nightfall, then it is best to say to them, "Fi arkoun", meaning "keep away, malicious one", in order to get them out of your way. Jewish women are integrated in three different dimensions: family, community and religion. Religion constitutes the primordial value system, followed by the community as opposed to the individual and then the family over the individual; thus, the North African individual who seeks a western psychotherapy has an entirely different *presence* from a western individual. Jewish women follow the laws of bodily purity, or *Nidda*, which govern their monthly life cycle and their world view; these laws relate to hygiene surrounding the menstrual cycle, pregnancy and labour; hence the importance of purification rites (ritual bath or *mikveh*) that are intended to remove every impurity from the body. The *Nidda* prescribe that spouses should be separated during the menstrual cycle to exclude any possibility of their having sexual relations or a level of intimacy during this period and the women of Constantine observed this separation like their sisters from other North African countries: sleeping in a separate bed, avoiding all physical contact and so on.

I must emphasise this bodily and emotional experience of young girls and married women, whose lives are structured by periods of purity and impurity and whose world views are deeply conditioned by this cultural and religious orientation. *Bedika* is an internal examination that then allows them to determine whether their period has ended. The term "period" [*règles*] is not in current usage since this is a western term; "impurity" is the word that is generally used. This being the case, the young adolescent girl confronts the emerging physiological and bodily change alone at the age of eleven to twelve years. I have heard reference to a ceremony held in some communities in which the members express their joy at welcoming a new potential mother among them. This kind of ceremony enables the young girl to experience all these bodily changes without any trauma. *The psychic preparation for women's future change of object*–that is, living with a man–is facilitated throughout the young girl's life by the practice of some favourite games. After this period of bodily change, more or less prepared by traditional rites of passage, the next stage for women is marriage; this is a major transition that involves many symbolic rites. To bring happiness to the marriage, the fish symbol is evoked; fish is eaten in order to make the marriage fertile, since the fish is associated with fertility. To bring happiness to the future wife, married women place seven bracelets on her arm and seven rings on her finger. This is known as the "beautiful hand" ritual and is based on the symbolic value of the figure seven, a belief that is also held by Muslims. In the Kabbalah, for example, the figure seven symbolises the man: seven is the product of adding three (the symbol of the soul) and four (the symbol of the body). Finally, there is the rite of the Mezuzah, or guardian of the threshold, which in addition to its traditional religious function as a reminder of the existence of God and the observance of his commandments, acts as a talisman to provide divine protection; the word *Shadday* (All-Powerful) appears in fact on the Mezuzah scroll. On the day of the wedding celebrations, the fiancé and fiancée go to bathe at different times at the *mikveh* (ritual bath). Three meanings are usually drawn from the water ritual, which signifies the source of life, purification and regeneration. During this bath, two rites are practised: first, some dried fruit is thrown into the bath as an offering to the djinns, for in North Africa these are thought to feed on blood, oil, feathers, couscous and dried fruit and giving them food is supposed to keep illnesses at bay. In the second rite, everything that floats to the surface of the bath (ears of wheat, eggshells, dried fruit) is collected, put in a small bag and placed under the mattress of the young married couple's bed. This rite is intended to bring happiness and, above all, fertility to the marriage. I have observed that the same procedures are used in other rituals that are intended to reverse a spell. During the marriage ceremony, the groom puts the ring on his wife's right index finger, which is considered to be the most active of the hand (reminiscent of Nina's deformed right index finger); the woman does not put any ring on the man. Finally, as the last protective rite of marriage, I shall describe the ritual performed just before the young married couple move into their new home: the evening before, small heaps of henna are placed in every room in the house, each with a lighted candle at its centre. This is a way of addressing the djinns that inhabit the place by begging them to give a favourable reception to the new occupants. The following day, a black rooster is sacrificed and its blood is sprinkled in the four corners of each room. The rooster and a dish of couscous is then prepared for the family and the neighbours to eat; then the leftovers are thrown in the well or the earth closet (Rouach, 1990).

Having described these cultural practices, I can now continue my account by introducing the other level on which the psychotherapy took place. The grandmother and her traditional methods were at work and this old witch-lady was operating in parallel with my treatment in her cultural frame of reference. It was only several years after this therapy began that I became aware of this fact through a change that occurred as I was listening. I sensed that the mourning was in progress: there was a change in Nina's attitude. She started to walk differently; instead of dragging herself along slowly rather like an "old woman", she became more dynamic, walking energetically in a way that seemed more fitting to her youth more. She smiled and took an interest in the patients in the waiting room; then she brought the following dream–again it was very short: "I dreamt that my father and my brother were in their coffins". For her, now, her father and her brother were dead and buried; she told me that she was not going to the graveyard so often and that she no longer followed her brother in all his wanderings. She preferred to walk around the department stores and buy clothes that she liked. Nina was seeing doctors less often and was coming regularly to all her sessions.

The transference relationship had facilitated a resurgence of life instincts and an orientation of the narcissistic libido; there was a recathexis of the body at least in the realm of external appearance. The violence of the hostile feelings that Nina was expressing towards her grandmother and, especially, towards the female doctor who was treating her at the hospital seemed to subside for a while, as if a particular stage had come to an end. In fact, for several years the female doctor had been blamed for the deformity of her finger following an injection. Consideration should also be given to the fragility of the bones in the context of this particular illness. It also seemed that the body was undergoing a somatic and emotional expression of symbolic prohibitions of oedipal castration that were not taken up by the psychic apparatus.

Nina had managed to involve all the members of her family in this hostile impulse, to the extent that a violent quarrel had driven the elder brother to confront the doctors in the hospital department. Needless to say, the doctors had some serious misgivings about continuing the treatment: it seemed to me that they were collectively and unconsciously becoming the bad objects or the intermediaries of the djinns! The foundations of this hostility revealed a shift from rivalry with her grandmother towards rivalry with her mother and siblings; in a dream from this period, Nina told me: "I dreamt about cockroaches; there were hundreds of them, the walls were black all over. I remember the wallpaper was black". In her associations, she talked about the people she had seen working to exterminate the insects in the city where she lived. The remaining content of the session was entirely devoted to her difficult relationships and quarrels with her brother (for the first time) and with her mother, to whom she did not dare to express her thoughts or feelings. In my view, this impulse heralded a transition towards a change of object. As the youngest family member, who was not working because of her illness, Nina had to take care of her aged mother and she felt sacrificed–in a Cinderella role. "I am my mother's prisoner; she has made me her companion, her friend and it's infuriating. I listen to her because she is old; I watch her to make sure she is breathing properly (desire and fear for her death) ... my brother and my sisters have never looked after her; my brother has never said to either my sister or me–"you go out, girls; I'll look after your mother". My mother can't hear and she can't walk properly; she too is alone!" As we can observe, the rivalry and the hostility projected on to the grandmother and the female doctor as omnipotent witches has shifted on to the mother and the brothers and sisters ("cockroaches to be eliminated"), a form of pest control!

Nina was finally able to confront the terrifying imago of her mother and mobilise her aggressive drives, which improved her state of health. This archaic imago was being modified, the oedipal and genital organisation was beginning to be established and the libido was slowly emerging from the pregenital stages.

When Nina talked about her deceased relatives it was to note the change but without any guilt: "We are going to the graveyard less often, which upsets me. When my father was alive, we went there for festivals; he must be saying "they've stopped thinking of me"; my elder brother said that he doesn't have time to take me there any more ... At home, the three of us are still sleeping in the same bedroom; we're still not sleeping in my brother's bedroom but this year we repainted it as he had wanted, with a *pink* padded bed [the colour pink from the anamnesis finally appears after all these years!] A stranger to the family asked: "Why is there an empty bedroom, one room for the living and another room for those who are no longer among the living?!" Answer: the three of us have got used to living together in the same bedroom".

Nina's health improved and her lupus erythematosus entered a remission phase; she was feeling better and her agoraphobic symptoms disappeared. These symptoms had emerged at her brother's death, revealing the displacement of oedipal sexual desires on to men she encountered in the street and confirming my hypothesis of an Oedipus complex centred on the brother and secondarily on the father. Nina's panic in the street was alleviated for years by the presence of her sisters or her brother, which averted the onset of anxiety. Moreover, Nina would sometimes snatch furtive glimpses from her window as through a *moucharabieh* (as in the harems) at the young people in the city; she seemed to be interested in one person in particular, but thought he might be too young for her. After all, though, wasn't one of her cousins going out with a younger man? It seemed to me that the pregenital problematic was diminishing and that she was embarking on a period of triangulation. I naïvely thought that the treatment was progressing and that the subsequent improvement must be attributed to this, but there were many events that raised problems and presented me with theoretical and methodological questions.

The healers' treatments

Nina was still feeling well and came to the room in which the psychotherapy was taking place with great agility and flexibility. She reported that she was pleased with the condition of her hands; the swelling had gone down and she no longer felt any stabbing pains–the pain seemed to have disappeared.

I wondered what might be the reason for this improvement and I put this question to Nina. She looked at me embarrassed, as if ashamed and told me awkwardly: "My brother recently drove a lady to a church in his taxi to make an offering to a saint and he encouraged me to go into this church" (the cult of saints again!) In doing this, she had felt some fear of entering this dark cave-like church and the desire to have hands that were not deformed–we should emphasise here the overdetermination of the cave, from the roofs of the rocks in the Rhumel river to the fertility cave of the springs from which the grandmother worked her cures and then to the cave-like church. Her brother accompanied her on this strange pilgrimage (hillula) and both made vows that their brother's murderers would be found and punished. Nina entered the church and touched the saint's statue with both her hands. She spoke to a young woman dressed in white who gave her a small stone to wear as a memento (an amulet?) Nina looked at me in some embarrassment ...

Secrets of the human race in the Maghreb

My patient's syncretism may be a cause for surprise; this transition from one set of religious practices to another can only be explained with reference to the following historical considerations. There are still very few studies that enable us to identify the common set of Judaeo-Berber beliefs and practices as opposed to the specific beliefs and practices of Jews of the Maghreb, as distinct from those of Judaism in the strict sense. These secrets are deeply interconnected with the history of the Jews in North Africa. I shall give a concise interpretation of this history, limited to the sociological elements that are necessary for explaining my theme.

The first element to consider is the *syncretism* that is a defining characteristic of the Jewish history of the Maghreb. Before becoming Christians and then Muslims, the Berbers were Jewish or Judaising. According to Ibn Khaldun, some Jews lived among the Shawia Berbers in Tamina and in the Tadla region on the Oum-er-Rbia River; the existence of some Jewish communities is also reported in the land of the Zenata Berbers in the far north in Gourara, between Tementit and Sba-Guerrara. It is these nomadic Jews who seem to have been responsible for the spread of Judaism beyond the Carthaginian domains. Leading the life of Bedouins, these Jews exerted a deep influence on the indigenous population, which practised a Judeo-Punic syncretism. Familiar with the Old Testament, these Judeo-Punics practised circumcision and existed "at the boundaries of Judaism, Christianity and primitive Paganism"; we encounter this particular aspect of North African Judaism, which continues to this day, in the proselytism of Jewish men who marry foreigners in the desire to convert them to Judaism. The "guer" or proselyte played an important role at this time and has done so ever since.

To this characteristic, I shall add another that is deeply revealing as to the cultural inclinations of North African Jews: the attachment to the Sepher-ha-Zohar or the Book of Splendour, which has gradually been accompanied by some practices that are far removed from Orthodox Judaism. Threatened by unstable political and economic conditions, the Jews in North African communities invoked the protection of God and the angels (Michael, Gabriel, Raphael and Uriel), whose names recur on every page of the Kabbalistic writings. However, this went further: the Zohar was used as an infallible remedy for protecting, treating, healing and so on; for example, it would be placed under the pillow of someone who was ill or an infertile woman. Some talismans were produced by printers: these were Hebrew prayers and Kabbalistic texts in Aramaic, written by renowned Kabbalists from North Africa and Israel. Their main purpose was to remove demonic influences from a man, or the dangers that might make him succumb to the *Aïn Ha-Ra*, or evil eye. They invoked the prophet Elijah, who struggled and overcame demonic spirits, whose names are revealed by the talismans. It was enough to inscribe these names for the demon spirit–the djinn–to be banished. To complete this sociological introduction to the defining characteristics of the Jewish people of North Africa, we must add to the syncretism and Kabbalistic practices the *cult of saints*.

The cult of saints clearly demarcates North African Judaism from European Judaism; it emerged under the influence of Islam. The boundaries are so fluid that Arab saints and *tsaddikim* receive offerings from the Jewish and Muslim populations without any distinction. This syncretism of two such austere monotheisms as Judaism and Islam is a further characteristic that has surprised more than one observer. The *tsaddik* and the marabout work miracle cures–for blindness, paralysis, "madness" and female infertility. Events in personal or family life–a marriage, a birth, a cure, a fulfilled wish or a death–can inspire the decision to make a pilgrimage to a saint's tomb. If certain witchcraft practices (*h'ttât*) have unleashed some mysterious destructive forces, these can be remedied by the *ziara* (pilgrimage). The pilgrim approaches the grave in a state of purity, removes his shoes, lights some candles, outstretches his hands towards the tomb, kisses the tombstone, places a piece of sugar on the stone, on to which he pours some water and then kneels to eat it. He recites psalms, says prayers for the peace of the saint's soul and prays for the fulfilment of the wish that has instigated his journey. On the anniversary of the saint's death or *hillula*, which means wedding in Aramaic, there is a group pilgrimage, with manifestations that combine spirituality and the return to ancestral practices. These manifestations have always found favour in rabbinic circles despite the fact that this is a practice very far removed from European Judaism and from the prescriptions of Moses. Despite the assimilation of French customs by North African Jews, it is very clear that the traditional practices endure.

Return to the commentary

When traditional practices come to light in the therapeutic process, it is important for the psychotherapist to create his own internal mental space for the expression of a particular psychic reality to which he has not become accustomed in his cultural frame of reference. This entails a cultural expansion of the therapeutic setting.

Following Nina's "pilgrimage" and her first confidences, I decided to make an intervention that would take account of this specific dimension. My observation was intended to reassure her and to establish a communication in the world of traditional approaches with which I was familiar but which we had never discussed. I therefore told her that I had known since the treatment began that her grandmother was a healer and that she herself believed in these practices. Reassured by my statement and my tacit approval of her pilgrimage to the church, which relieved her sense of guilt, Nina told me about an event in her recent past: "Two years ago, my grandmother spent two days with me; she made me drink some fluids, put some objects [healing objects?] under my bed, then went to the edge of a river in the countryside to throw some "things" into it; my grandmother died later that year ..." Nina continued the session by talking about the improvement in the treatment of her illness–she had reduced the high dose of cortisone by 5 mg daily–and she told me in passing that one of her brother's presumed murderers had been found dead, having drowned in a river (confirming her grandmother's power).

In parallel with my therapeutic treatment, a traditional therapy was taking place in a form of lateral transference but, more importantly, in another universe. Is this dual approach to be recommended when treating a patient who bestrides two cultural worlds?

After this crucial session, the therapy seemed to change course and Nina spoke: "I used to have pretty hands with a ring on every finger; the women were jealous of me. I was young and pretty and, then, with my illness, my hands became deformed".

"Do you think you were the victim of a curse?" "Yes, eight or nine years ago now, my Maghrebian neighbour who lived in the flat below told me after my brother died that he was a bad man"–her neighbour had thus destroyed or tried to destroy Nina's honourable image of her brother as a respectable merchant who had draped her in fur coats and jewels during his lifetime. The brother's presents were very out of keeping with the family's modest standard of living and this puzzled the rest of the family. For unknown reasons, this woman had cursed and threatened her: "I will send a man after you to threaten and follow you". "Who was this woman?" "This woman was a 'witch'. She had lots of men to visit her and burnt incense all day long".

This was the first emergence of the sexual dimension with an omnipotent woman (a witch, emulator of Lilith) who seduced many men and displayed an abundant sexuality with which Nina felt in rivalry, but in a pregenital mode characteristic of Lilith. Nina thought that this woman was jealous of her jewels and her ring-covered hands: "*Aïn Ha-Ra*"! Nina was a pretty young woman with deformed hands who served her family; her hands bore witness to this curse. During another session, Nina addressed the story of her birth; her mother had been three months pregnant when boarding the boat that took them to France. They had then lived in the grand-mother's flat, which accommodated her eight children and their families. Nina's family had lived in the kitchen. At her birth, which had taken place with some difficulties(?), her grandmother had uttered the following words on looking at the newborn baby: "Throw her away; throw your child away!" The grandmother's strange words first reminded me of an African cultural reference concerning the newborn baby's witch identity and the threat that it posed to the family. Was this the case for Nina? With her knowledge of the future, had the grandmother guessed that the baby had a witch identity, with all the dangers that this entailed for the family? *Tamgart enni teshart tamoqurant*, as the Berbers say: "That old lady [grandmother] was a great witch". What is the situation then with a witch child or baby? Or had Nina been possessed from birth by a djinn because the family lived in contact with the water in the kitchen, the favourite element of the djinns?!

What mattered here throughout all my interpretations was the psychodynamic role that these beliefs played in my patient's imagination. We then entered a new phase in the therapy.

Progress in parallel: psychosomatic therapy and traditional healing

The psychotherapy then continued in a transference atmosphere of remarkable trust: Nina said that I was truly different from the doctors she usually saw; "yes, it's true that you're not like these doctors, you're like us", meaning the members of this family. She had been a pretty baby and her grandmother and great-grandmother had grown so fond of her that their daughters, her aunts and great-aunts, were jealous (reminiscent of fairy tales). During the year that followed this therapeutic change, she gave me the following information: "Fourteen years ago my grandmother spent three days with me performing a ceremony to get rid of my lupus. She put something under my bed, then we got into a car and went to the edge of a faraway lake to throw something into it, but it didn't work".

I think that it was fear of the "evil eye" (mine) on the benefits of her grandmother's treatment that made Nina tell me "it didn't work", which is behaviour that accords with the cultural tradition. My immediate interpretation of her grandmother's healing act suddenly opened for me the gates of my past and the countertransference impulse.

When I was fifteen years old and suffering from some sight problems that were worsening, my mother had taken me to an ophthalmologist. He found a disease in the cornea that would ultimately lead to blindness. This news made a dramatic impact on me because it dashed all my hopes of studying medicine, to say nothing of the horrible thought of living in the dark for the rest of my days. I was treated with the medicine of the time in the hope that this would slow down the illness and prevent it from developing. It was then that my mother surprised me; she was someone who firmly embraced modernity but had some traditional attitudes concerning the observance of local festivals and culinary traditions. However, there was another dimension of which I had been unaware; one day, she arranged for a visit from a Muslim woman who brought a small cauldron (*quannoun*) that was used in the countryside for keeping warm in winter, as well as for cooking meals. I was curious and at the same time I was quietly anxious: what was going to happen? Who was this woman? Had she come here for my sake? My mother and this healer talked in Arabic and my mother left the room and returned with a piece of lead, "*khfif*". The witch melted the lead in a container that she held over the small cauldron and, once it was molten, she began to interpret the strange shape formed by the lead. She then showed it to both me and my mother; she then asked her for a glass of water and to my great surprise threw it in my face, giving me a shock. Then the two women continued their conversation in Arabic and the "healer" left without looking at me! This description accords with the customary behaviours of traditional healers. That night I had a dream that I will remember to the end of my days: two women in my family were present and one of them picked up a knitting needle that she pushed into my eye. Since that time, having also continued to take the medicine, my illness has not developed any further.

The problem with using two parallel forms of treatment–medical treatment and traditional healing practices–lies in the attribution of efficacy. Which of the two treatments had worked or had they both? Should we even formulate the problem in these terms?

How are we to interpret the therapeutic progress? In *L'influence qui guérit* [The healing influence] (1994, p. 141), Tobie Nathan established the conceptual framework for traditional therapies in terms of:

1. Propositions stated in *narrative* form, so that, for example, "the healer's personal history often constitutes one of the narratives of reference. When it is told, according to manifestly encoded forms, it functions as a sort of mythical matrix that constitutes the container both for the pathology of the patients and for the form of therapy that will be applied to them". This narrative exerts a deep influence on the patient's psychic apparatus and "imposes a series of reorganisations".

2. The use of *therapeutic operators*; that is, "logical procedures induced by the therapist that bring serious pressures to bear on the patient (his thought, action, organisation)"; Nathan identifies three of these operators: reversal, mediation and analogy.

The basic hypothesis is that some djinns, through either their own action or manipulation by malevolent people, enter the bodies of innocent people and cause various illnesses—somatic or mental afflictions or both. "Healing the patient consists in removing these from him" ... having inscribed the patient's pathology in the logic of his imaginative topography (i.e. demonology), the healer's skill consists in demonstrating ... a reversal process, forcing the patient to reverse the pathological logic in his turn"; if the djinns have entered, they can also come out.

In Nina's case, as in my own, the healers sought to reverse the processes in order to work the cure. Nina's grandmother used a procedure known to the Berber witches of Kabylia, known as *settut*: "For an ulcer or a tumour or [the illness from which Nina was suffering] ... take some blood, nail clippings and hair from the person who is ill, wrap them in a knotted cloth and attach them to a river bed"; this method was recorded by Edmond Doutté (1984) in Attia, a village near Constantine. This operation is thought to purge the illness and wash it away, as running water would. All these practices are based on the premise that a part of the body or an object that has been in contact with the body can substitute for it and that, if these are subjected to certain processes, the body from which they come will be affected in the same way.

These principles are cited by Fraser, to whose work Freud refers in *Totem and Taboo*. Accordingly, the two conditions of the traditional healing act are, first, a similarity or connection between the material that is worked on and the patient's body and, second, an observed resemblance between the behaviour of the material and the patient's body. These two conditions are identical to the process of *association of ideas* and, above all, to the analogical form: "Just as ... so". Just as river water can help us to wash, it can also help to wash away the illness from which we are suffering. From the use of analogical reasoning by healers of every persuasion, Tobie Nathan infers a further characteristic of therapeutic operators: "They tend to trigger inexplicable processes–such as analogical reasoning–that have enduring effects long after the first induction and even in the healer's absence" (Nathan, 1994, p. 151).

Let us return briefly to the procedure to which I was subjected, which re-emerged in the context of the countertransference. This is a therapeutic reversal through the emergence of meaningful shapes (strange forms in the molten lead) with a view to transforming the pathology: a witch's attack giving rise to hypotheses never communicated by my mother as to a possible attack by a close family member. Despite my mother's silence, a dream came to compensate for the lacking words and in particular thoughts during the cauldron procedure—a dream that indicated that unconsciously I had someone in mind! I had never since thought about that episode that took place around 45 years ago. In the course of some research, I chanced(?) on the following text quoted by Doutté: "To afflict an enemy's eyes. Take a candle and mould it into the image of the person you want to attack, write the seven signs on it with your enemy's name and his mother's name and gouge out both eyes of this figurine with two spikes [This is strangely reminiscent of my dream about a woman gouging out my eye]. Then put it in a pot with some quicklime, having thrown on a bit of *chârib el h'amâm and* bury it right next to the fire" (1984, p. 299).

During my own analysis, I was able in another space (my psychoanalysis) to interpret this distant dream by pursuing a different track, linking castration fantasy and the parental relationship, but I still have some inner questions about this memorable scene: did the *settut* cure me? Do I owe the arrested development of this illness to its effect or to that of the medicine? I shall leave these questions unanswered, in the knowledge that these distant memories enable me to maintain internally the connections with my childhood ego.

After this session, there was a deep change in the therapeutic atmosphere; when Nina talked about me as a psychotherapist, she included me in the tribal "we": "You're like us". She then continued to make recourse to traditional practices; with her upstairs neighbour, she had gone to see a marabout (a very long way away!) and he had made a love potion to bring her closer to a young man to whom her deceased brother had introduced her–a distant cousin with whom she had fallen in love.

In his remarkable book, completed in 1908, Edmond Doutté reproduced in enormous detail some rituals and other traditional procedures used to treat or influence other people. I shall quote from this book the ritual for inspiring love, which I think Nina's marabout may have used: "Take a piece of earth that has been under the feet of the person whose feelings you want to influence and some of his hair, as well as a small piece of his clothing; put the earth in this piece of cloth and tie it up with the hair while reciting the names of the moon seven hundred times. The operation must be performed at the time of Venus, under the constellation of Taurus, on a Wednesday; after every hundred names recited, say: "O, such a person, grant your love to such a person, as Zuleika loved Joseph, all homage to him! On you, I throw the love (*mah'abba*) and raging fire of passion". As soon as you have finished these incantations, cense with some olibanum; then bury the knotted cloth in a stranger's grave. The love will only grow between the woman and the man following this procedure".

Nina claimed that this didn't work! Was this really true? The reader must understand the power of the belief in the "evil eye", even with people who are trusted. She then told me about another matter of the heart that had also been less than successful: she had been supposed to marry another young man, who was tall, strong and obese and who had lost some weight in order to please her. This was at the time when she had had the operation on her right-hand index finger and this young man had come to visit her in hospital, but out of pride she had sent him away for ever. We should remember that her father and her elder brother were similarly corpulent, as was her grandmother's husband; this connection again reveals the strong presence of the oedipal prohibition and her gradual transition towards the change of object.

I posed Nina the following question: what have you done with this finger? I was thinking about the overdetermination of this symptom, which represents the punishment of autoerotic practices and symbolic castration. Instead of answering me, she posed me a question as to the day on which a pilgrimage should be made to the graveyard (this was her own–very oriental–way of associating). Now, the operation on her finger and its deformity followed her brother's death, as if in self-punishment for her incestuous desire towards her brother. We thus return to Nina's castration complex and pregenital fixation, since she saw herself as a woman who was dangerous to men.

Nina had remained in the image of the sirens and North African *settut*, "anti-women" who are dangerous to men; that is, women who have not yet accomplished the detachment from the original maternal object and directed their libido towards another object; this was the problem of transition encountered by Lilith, the first mother and phallic mother, to Eve, the genital mother. To my knowledge, these two imagos have never yet been used by psychoanalysts to describe the transition from pregenitality to genitality.

Nina returned to the subject of her birth and her early years of family life in her grandmother's kitchen and I then thought that her mother must have been depressive during her pregnancy and in the months following the birth. We know that the immune system is established at the end of the first year of life and the question arises as to what effect this might have had on the immune system and early relations between mother and baby? Were there not in fact some difficult conditions in the maternal and family environment underlying Nina's fragility? There had been the emigration, her mother's depression and the reactivation of the depressive family atmosphere at the move into a district of Paris, which had severed the family from its community and tribal roots. *I am advancing the hypothesis of an essential depression involving a progressive disorganisation with long-term emergence of the lupus erythematosus.*

Nina had constructed an entire novel about her origins; as a child, she had been fair-skinned with long blonde curly hair and so different from her brothers and sisters that they would "wind her up" by telling her that she was not their sister; they were from Algeria, whereas she was French. Nina described her grandmother's flat, in particular a locked room in which her grandmother kept her treasures: bags of money–a description worthy of Ali Baba's cave. However, despite her riches this woman had not helped Nina's father, who had lived in poverty with his family. "My father was generous; he gave everything to the poor". Nina loved bags and would spend her time buying them. This was a way of identifying with her grandmother whom she admired and, at the same time, gaining some narcissistic reinforcement. The atmosphere of the sessions changed substantially; Nina was more at ease and talked to me in confidence. She continued to progress and the illness no longer seemed to be developing–there was a remission phase. Nina now wanted to attend to her body. She was in fact very hesitant about going to see a surgeon to treat her deformed hands. She made the appointments herself, met the surgeon and fixed the date for the operation. She talked about this in every session; she was afraid, but she wanted to change and she particularly wanted to prevent her elder brother getting involved in this. Her attitude towards him was changing; he would come into the three women's flat and behave as if he were at home, but she made it clear to him that this was not his territory. She fully realised that her brother was often depressed and she no longer wanted to join him in his Parisian wanderings.

Nina criticised her female doctor at the hospital: "Mrs X is not like us [referring to herself and me]; she isn't treating me effectively–she doesn't know what's wrong with me". I replied: "What do you think your illness is?" (I had long thought that she had a mental representation of her illness that differed from the medical description and she confirmed this). "You think she is a bad doctor, as if she were a bad mother for you!" "She's not like us, I'm losing my hair because of her; it's because of her that my finger is deformed because she's the one who gave me the injection; it is she who has made me ill. I would like to have a kind woman as a doctor; then I would be able to call her at home. I found one in the same hospital but she refuses to treat me because it is not done to take a colleague's patients".

This implication of the doctor who was treating her and the projection of hostile feelings towards her originated from her mother's recent hospitalisation for a heart condition and her fear for her life. However, her mother's life was not in danger; on the contrary, looking after her all day was increasing Nina's hostile feelings and her lassitude. She dared not criticise her mother or show her any anger; her only solution was to accuse her doctor and turn her into a bad mother. The charges against the European doctors kept mounting, because Nina cited many examples of bad treatment of close family members, concluding that the European doctors were in fact bad healers. Also, Nina had recently met a young Maghrebian woman whom she had known in hospital three years earlier. This woman had told her that she had had a marvellous ointment from a Middle Eastern country sent over as a treatment (a traditional remedy, of course) and this ointment had cured her. Nina looked at me as if to ask for my approval; I advised her to try it!

At one of the last few sessions, Nina arrived looking completely changed, as if her appearance were beginning to reveal more of her sexuality. I interpreted this new way of being as a good sign. She continued her diatribe against the doctors and this time against the surgeon, whom she said addressed her in an over-familiar way. "Of course, if I were a tall, beautiful, rich, aristocratic woman, perhaps I would be given good treatment! The doctors are not effective; for this I would have to be richer. If I were an attractive woman, I would be cured".

At the last session, Nina looked very elegant. She was closer now to Eve than to Lilith. She was approaching another stage of her life; it was time to consider bringing the therapeutic process to an end. This is always a difficult decision for the psychotherapist.

Clinical and theoretical propositions concerning the psychotherapeutic process with somatic patients

We can now begin to sum up the recommendations for psychosomatic psychotherapies, as follows.

- A benevolent and empathetic attitude on the part of the psychotherapist, alternating between mental closeness and distance in a way that enables the patient's psychic functioning to be assessed.

- Providing a protective shield in terms of attitude and role to safeguard the patient in the session setting from overwhelming excitations that would jeopardise his somatic equilibrium.

- A face-to-face relationship (armchair to armchair), presenting the psychotherapist in his sensorimotricity, facilitating the identification process and, at the same time, a psychic reinvigoration (Marty, 1990).

- Facilitating the psychic cathexis of the apparatus for thinking thoughts.

- Working in a team with the doctors who are treating the patient to avert any risk of a sudden relapse or somatisation at critical points in the therapeutic process.

- Assisting the resumption of psychic functioning (constitution of the preconscious) and creating the mental space for expressing the violence of the aggressive drives.

Specific proposals concerning the children of immigrants living in France

In the European environment in which they have grown up, the children of migrants present some complex problems that cannot be addressed by a European psychoanalyst, armed only with his classical experience and practical expertise. After many years of treating patients who are foreign to the western universe and having studied some ethnopsychoanalytic works, I would like to conclude this research study by presenting some proposals for the consideration of therapists regardless of their origin.

First, as concerns indications and contra-indications for psychoanalysis and psychoanalytically based techniques, I think that these are contra-indicated for first-generation immigrants and require adjustment for second-generation immigrants. With second-generation immigrants, on the other hand, the therapeutic approach is difficult and even an adjustment of psychoanalytic technique may not be adequate for treating such patients. Why is this? As we have seen with Nina, in parallel with the psychoanalytically based psychosomatic treatment, some traditional practices were being followed at the patient's family and cultural level. Until I became aware of this dimension, the two universes existed separately in parallel and a large part, if not most, of the patient's psychological and emotional life was inaccessible to the treatment. This presents the psychotherapist with several problems, as follows.

• Knowledge of the patient's cultural frame of reference

Without this knowledge no interpretation is possible, as could be observed in the diagnosis made by the referring doctor. In this respect, the nosographic categories should be revised, for the richness of the imagination in these patients can be assessed only with a preliminary knowledge of the myths and cultures of their universe.

• Countertransference analysis

There are several aspects to countertransference analysis, depending on the therapist's identity. If the therapist is a western European, he will have to overcome the impediment of the defence mechanisms associated with the prevailing rationalist scientific approach because, although he may be able to give some coherence to unconscious psychic phenomena in European patients with the same cultural and mythological background, it is a different matter with immigrant patients. Moreover, this therapist will have to confront some hostility from his colleagues (accusations of encouraging magic practices, animistic thinking and so on, which may ultimately undermine his status as a psychoanalyst!). Finally, he will have to overcome all his own inner hostility towards differences that may either attract him or, more commonly, activate his aggressive impulses of rejection.

However, if the therapist is a European who combines several cultures including some outside Europe, or if he is the descendant of a non-European immigrant who has lived in Europe for many years, perhaps following some studies, the problem will resemble that of the case I have described. This will involve a return to the constitutive sources of his psychic life, including all the difficulties associated with the acquisition of western culture, which will act as an insuperable barrier. In fact, this hazardous path involves feelings of shame and guilt, as it will entail a cultural clash in the psyche between the values acquired in the family and values acquired at school and university, quite apart from the institutional ego ideal of psychoanalytic societies. This involves a journey of initiation that is identical to that taken by initiates among the ancient peoples of the earth, which can be undertaken alone or in the company of others; that is, by joining groups that study and discuss cultural differences. The solitary path is difficult and uncertain and the therapist is at risk of losing and harming his patients.

I shall not discuss the case of immigrant therapists who have never severed their roots and are therefore working within the context of their traditions; it would be helpful to be able to learn about their reflections and experiences from some publications.

• Kinship relations

Kinship relations are one of the elements to be considered in the therapeutic indication. In *The Elementary Structures of Kinship* (1977), Claude Lévi-Strauss points the way; the individual person who turns to us as therapists belongs to a complex relational system, which is ignored at peril of leading the treatment to an impasse. The patient is not an individual in the European sense but a member of a family group, a tribe and so on. As we observed, Nina, who would sometimes still refer to herself in the first person plural, was the spokeswoman for her family and often her tribe. Should the relational technique be adjusted? In what way? I see two dimensions to this problematic.

First, we must give very serious consideration to the risk that the therapeutic process will ultimately separate the patient from his immediate environment, as a result of the dynamics of the European identity process. In the best case, the patient will harmoniously combine his cultures of belonging and adoption and will be better adapted to European city life, although there may be some loss of quality in his family relationships. This is an important risk that should not be overlooked.

Second, to preserve the family and tribal homeostasis, we may want to consider meeting family members at the patient's request and in his presence. We should also be able to respond to any anxious questions they may have about the therapeutic process, as well as make a mental adjustment to the therapeutic space to incorporate the role played by the patient's illness in the family equilibrium, which is closer to techniques used in family therapy.

- Imagination

The imagination of second-generation immigrants is constituted in two ways. First, it incorporates all the family's mental representations, inherited from cultures of origin: education and transmission of customs, eating habits, behaviours in everyday life and, above all, founding myths. Just as Europeans have their myths of reference, so do the other peoples of the earth. We all know the importance of Greek mythology for European civilisation and for the structuring of the psyche. However, for reasons of intellectual concision and ethnocentrism, European psychoanalysts have claimed to find in all the world's civilisations the founding myths of their own civilisation, which they have elevated as a civilisation of reference for reasons of economic success. In the context of a conclusion, it would be impossible to review the numerous controversies surrounding the universality of psychoanalytic concepts.

However, would it not be possible to adapt this approach in order to investigate the founding myths that lie at the origin of the psychic functioning of the world's peoples? This would mean dealing with some myths that are much more ancient and very different from those of Ancient Greece. Thus, Nina has helped us to retrace the path of Adam's first wife, Lilith. This first female figure of humanity, who is unknown to some or thought to have disappeared for ever, is alive and well. She occupies the thoughts and influences the behaviour of several hundred million of the world's inhabitants from the Canary Islands to the borders of Pakistan. With her children, the invisible creatures known as djinns, she is present in their daily lives; she reveals this at all the crucial points in their existence: birth, initiation, marriage, death and all the festivals. This example gives pause for reflection on the formidable presence of the founding myths of humanity.

From my own experience, the thought of Lilith inspires greater anxiety than the thought of the Sphinx from Greek mythology, although it has been familiar to me from my earliest childhood. The djinns had a presence that Zeus and the seductive sirens of the beloved Ulysses never had.

It will thus become clearer why the second constituent of mental representations in a "transplanted" individual has a weaker intensity of drive cathexis than representations from the archaic constitution of the psyche, since it involves a set of representations from a later constitution.

Traditional beliefs and customs form the basis of the systems of mental representations in peoples living outside Europe. As a result of their codification, these are often similar from one person to the next so that on a first impression they can appear identical. There are individual variations in each person's experience but it is true that the shared cultural background is sufficiently powerful to create the impression of a uniform and even a simple world view. I would immediately discourage any thought of this kind because this is a highly complex universe with origins dating back to the beginning of time. The repressed material and the nature of the forces of repression are radically different.

• Psychoanalysis and cultural difference

The reflections that I am now putting forward concur with intellectual trends that have arisen in psychoanalytic circles during research into cultural differences. Freud's thought proves truly universal when it demonstrates how, from one individual to another, adaptive and regulatory impulses emerge and combine from imaginative components common to all humanity according to the context of the time, organising not only a necessary and ever provisional equilibrium between narcissistic cathexes and object cathexes but, more importantly, an integration of the narcissistic cathexes–thus initially violent–within the object cathexes–thus essentially libidinal.

For Freud, psychogenesis is explained by the primordial and universal role played by infantile sexuality and the vagaries of mental functioning appear to depend on various equally universal reference-points proposed by Freudian metapsychology. Freud's explanatory procedure is then structured on the basis of the oedipal model that he understands to exist in all cultures and, in particular, the castration anxiety and repression that stem from this universal Oedipus complex.

To amplify Freud's propositions, it should be said that much of his thought is based on the postulate of the organisational primacy of the Oedipus complex, conceived from the outset as triangular and genital; this organisation is universal and accords with all the facts of culture worldwide. This being said, what are the stages in the organisation of the human psyche that precede the Oedipus complex but are equally universal, which have not been integrated into the model but are of prime importance in defining the psychic functioning specific to somatic patients?

According to Bergeret (1993), we must carefully study Freud's text on "transference neuroses", which was discovered in 1983 and was to form the twelfth chapter of the work on metapsychology. This text illustrates Freud's misgivings concerning universal facts that would mark the onset of human affective functioning, considered from the metaphorical perspective of phylogenesis. The other truth proclaimed by the Oedipus myth as a whole is the violence that plays an important role in the earliest relations between the adult and what we are now finally concerned with as the "baby", as distinct from the "child". This text of Freud's reveals the dynamic and topographical consequences of *a truly narcissistic organisation considered to exist at the beginning of universal ontogenesis*. He demonstrates that a violent instinct, originally conceived as entirely natural and in no sense aggressive, slightly precedes the libido in its organising effect on the personality. It can be observed that in this text Freud addresses the theme of primitive instinctual violence without any reference to an already active Oedipus complex. There are two references concerning violence: one is the threat posed to the son's life in the context of oedipal rivalry, which is therefore already erotised violence; the other is pure narcissistic violence.

Like many of his contemporaries, Freud hesitates to discuss matricide or infanticide; *clinical practice has demonstrated the frequency of infanticidal fantasies in young mothers. During the investigations described in this work, I have frequently emphasised either affective deficiency in mothers, or the fact that the children were not wanted by one or both of their parents.* We are dealing with imaginative representations that are painful but universal. It is necessary to reconsider the sources of the structuring of the somatopsychic organisation that combines the omnipotence of both father and mother; that is, an absolute potential that is not yet sexually differentiated. Its main characteristic remains in the register of phallic rather than genital power. "The narcissistic organisation" and the varieties of pregenital development are the psychic structures required for the psychic development of somatic patients.

Although the Oedipus complex is the acme of psychosexual development, there is some obscurity surrounding the topographical, economic and dynamic conditions that correspond to the beginnings of relational functioning. My argument in favour of a primary economic organisation that constitutes the beginnings of every psychic organisation, based on my clinical practice, the works of psychosomaticians and Bergeret's works on fundamental violence, is intended to emphasise its role in the context of theory and practice.

As we may recall, "Apollo tells Laius and Jocasta as future parents that the earliest affective communications between children and parents are dominated by the natural survival instinct present on both sides. Accordingly, there is no place in the sun for two—for both child and adult. This anxiety appears to be reciprocal and affects father and mother, as well as son and daughter. Thus Oedipus should have been killed on Mount Cithaeron; that is the universal potential fantasmatic destiny of every child in the world. Later, having killed his father, Oedipus kills his mother twice; first the phallic mother in the form of the sphinx (Lilith), then the genital mother" (Bergeret, 1993, p. 829).

• Attitudes towards healers

The psychotherapy of a second-generation immigrant, as we have seen in Nina's case, takes place on two levels: the psychoanalytic level and the traditional healing level. This is a different problem from that of a lateral transference; the psychotherapist either completely ignores the existence of the traditional dimension and fails to make progress with his patient or he accepts this dimension, deeply respects it and does not interpret the traditional approach in psychoanalytic terms because that would amount to a blatant attack on the constituents of the patient's psyche, striking at the very foundations of his homeostasis. In this respect, this type of patient is in serious danger faced with a psychoanalyst who wants his skills to triumph, since he will only replicate the well-known situation of the coloniser and the colonised.

I shall follow the recommendations made to me by two of my mentors–one in psychoanalysis, Sacha Nacht, the other in psychosomatics, Pierre Marty: "Always respect your patients' spiritual or religious beliefs; do not attempt to modify this domain". It seems that the traditional therapeutic process occurs in the realm of the coenaesthetic organisation that is located at the origins of the somatopsychic and our approach can only register the improvement in our patients due to the combined action of the healers and our therapy. It goes without saying that our narcissism may have to suffer in the process, which is an injury that needs to be overcome. Accepting the existence of this specific dimension constitutes a remarkable therapeutic lever for the psychotherapist, which brings benefits in the transference and a relationship of increased trust.

The theoretical discussion thus far has led us to a better understanding of the influence of healers' actions on the first organisation at the borders of the psyche; the patients thus benefits from a substantial narcissistic reinforcement that brings a resurgence in the life instincts, as Pierre Marty would say. This is the hypothesis that I am putting forward concerning traditional practices; we should remember that traditional therapies are still practised by the majority of peoples on the earth.

Conclusion

"This is the great error of our day in the treatment of the human body, that physicians separate the soul from the body", Plato, *Chronicle 156c.*

It is time to put an end to the psyche-soma division that was generated by the founders of medicine and psychoanalysis and to follow Plato's recommendations.

Might over a century of progress in various disciplines, including the neurosciences, make it possible to remove the epistemological barrier that Freud constructed in order to create psychoanalysis? The present work forms part of the contemporary trend towards the unification and interrelation of disciplinary fields with a view to explaining somatisation processes in the light of malfunctionings in the psychic apparatus and to proposing a general approach to patients and their illnesses in conjunction with doctors. In the process, I have been confronted with some formidable epistemological problems. First of all, there was the problem of the status of the psychic apparatus in relation to all the levels of the living organism; it follows from the removal of the epistemological hiatus that the psychic apparatus must form part of the living organism not as a spatially materialised function but, in contrast to the metapsychological approach, as an immaterial function that cannot be located in the body.

In order to facilitate the representation of this subjective functioning that belongs to the "soft sciences",[34] I shall propose that doctors and psychologists think about their patients using the image of the "world wide web", a vast network of entirely interconnected communication that facilitates communication between subsystems and their functional autonomy while ultimately taking account of all the changes that have occurred. Moreover, this network enables users to make contact at long distance and to create "virtual fora" for solving problems or exchanging information. This mode of virtual reality seems to bear many similarities with the mode of functioning in living organisms. We understand that this visual analogy can help us to perceive the interrelations between the three dimensions that I have emphasised throughout this work, namely the investigation of somatic disorders that need to be understood in connection with psychic disorders and the sources of disorders that originate from the environment. Thought is not transcendent; it is deeply connected with bodily, neuronal and psychic functions. As Edelman and Damasio observed, we think and we feel with the body.

The clinical experience I have obtained over the last five years in various medical departments at the hospital has strongly convinced me that the place of a psychoanalyst-psychosomatician is among his doctor colleagues and that he must act in dynamic interrelation with them. The regrettable absence of psychology and psychoanalysis courses in medical faculties, combined with deficiencies in the practice of investigating the "psychological" dimension in patients, provides sufficient evidence of the case for such a resource. I remember the request made by a young intern after the meeting of medical staff that I attended; she wanted me to communicate my practical expertise in investigating patients so that she could improve her medical practice. This observation is reminiscent of Balint's endeavours concerning the doctor-patient relationship. I think that this was a first step, but we must extend scientific collaboration further; teams of psychologists should work alongside medical staff to give the care necessary for a fundamental good psychic functioning to assist in the improvement of health, if not the cure itself. I have often seen patients, partly cured in medical terms, returning to these departments three or four months later. In the face of family or professional problems, the same processes of regression or disorganisation as those described above are reactivated to instigate the emergence of somatic symptoms that are perceptible to doctors: *the body displaces the mind.*

There is a serious discrepancy between clinical practice based on collaboration between practitioners from various disciplines and studies intended to establish the interrelation of fields that are still a long way apart. Recent studies in psychobiology, stress medicine and the neurosciences, as well as studies by neuropsychoanalysts such as Mark Solms, Jaak Panksepp and Vilanayur Ramachandran, Daniel Stern, David Olds, Robert Galatzer-Lévy, are paving the way for a discipline that has yet to be founded; there is still a very long way to go. This is the reason why multidisciplinary clinical practice in hospitals seems to me to be the most appropriate way forward to pursue and develop.

Everything depends on a new medical approach with theoretical and clinical dimensions that can restore the connection between psychoanalysis and biology.

APPENDICES

Appendix I: Table of Fundamental Structures

1. Table of fundamental structures developed by J. B. Stora based on P. Marty's "Mouvements individuels de vie et de mort" [Individual life and death impulses], T1 and T2 [5] [6] (also published in *Annales de psychiatrie*, Vol. 10, No. 1. 1995–"Organisations mentales et maladies somatiques" [Mental organisations and somatic diseases]).

	Classical mental neuroses (p. 111) (ref. S. Freud)	Well-mentalised neuroses (p. 121) (ref. P. Marty)	Neuroses with uncertain mentalisation (p. 122) (ref. P. Marty)	Poorly mentalised neuroses (p. 123) (ref. P. Marty)	Behavioural neuroses (p. 131) (ref. P. Marty)
Characteristics	Classical field of psycho-analytic studies Obsessional neuroses/ phobic neuroses		Concern the majority of the contemporary population	Concern the majority of the contemporary population	Structural diagnosis cannot be established without an analysis of the entire personality rather than from behaviours. Behaviours involve no form of structure.
Topographies	Second topography/ well organised and maintained systems of mental defence	Both topographical systems are in constant motion. Stable organisation of second phase of the anal stage. Less well organised and maintained systems of mental defence.	Lack of stable organisation of second phase of the anal stage. Questionable authenticity of the superego.	First topography (Ucs/Pcs/Cs) subject to disorganisations Functions irregularly over time.	Unstable functioning of the first topography. Failure of the anal genetic organisation. No constitution of the oedipal superego. Lack of common central fasciculus. Lack of mental elaboration.
Representations	Representations with psychic depth and breadth. Representations relating to the anal organisation (retention and mastery).	Easy representations/ fluidity, substance and constancy.	Variations in preconscious functioning. Representations and associations variable over time: Sometimes rich, at other times poor and superficial.	Few or no representations, superficial, with few associations.	Representations accessible to consciousness. Behaviours and conduct arising directly from the unconscious.

173

Appendix II: Mathematical Model: Trauma, Quantity of Excitations and Long-term Development of Psychic Energy Behaviours

Proposal for a simplified explanatory model of fluctuations in psychic energy according to the quantity of endogenous and exogenous excitations induced by a traumatic event.

A human being's biological and psychic life unfolds in a complex dynamic environment to which he is subject and which interacts with his own endogenous rhythms–these are rhythms of the respiratory system, the heart, the cortex, sleep, the stomach, the metabolism, the psychic economy (connected with vital and libidinal tonus) and so on. The stability of these rhythms is a particularly urgent issue because the human being as a subject can influence them through his behaviours, thoughts and emotions. All these rhythms are synchronised but they can be disrupted by life events (such as illnesses or behavioural and emotional reactions) and it is therefore important to be able to work as effectively as possible to predict their developments and to intervene in the interest of patients. In the observations in Chapters 1, 2, 3 and 4, I have sought on a speculative basis to demonstrate oscillations in psychic energy and their transmission to the somatic realm, with the consequent disruptions, as well as the resumptions of psychic life that attenuate and stabilise the somatic control systems. The body and the psyche take over in turn but, when the psychic apparatus finally gives way, it is the somatic control systems that protect the vital equilibria, which are stabilised by various medical interventions.

We are confronted with oscillators, internal clocks that are themselves the result of complex regulatory processes; living organisms have the natural ability to work at different rhythms, hence the theoretical difficulty of comparing this to the functioning of a single oscillator. Research into the fibrillation of cardiac muscle has demonstrated that this activity illustrates the breakdown of a collective synchronisation between a large number of oscillators: "Every cardiac muscle fibre can be regarded as an oscillator that beats periodically in normal functioning and this period is the same for all fibres when these are strongly coupled. The general behaviour can then create the illusion of a single oscillator but when, for reasons as yet unknown, this coupling ceases to operate, the cardiac cells act independently of each other and spatio-temporal disorder inevitably ensues" (Bergé, Pomeau & Dubois-Gance, 1997, p. 183).

The dynamics of the living organism thus reveal that stimuli can generate very different responses according to the specific time. Because they are interrelated, oscillators can be synchronised through complex processes such as those of "synchronisers": a set of physical factors–lighting, temperature, food and so on with periodic variations that can bring about a period close to their own in biological rhythms, such as rhythms of sleep, temperature and hormonal activities in general. It would thus seem that human beings, just like simple clocks whose frequencies change when they are stimulated by an external oscillation, only regain their internal stability at the cessation of the external activity. This is a long way removed from Claude Bernard's concept of a stable point of homeostasis; observing the presence of periodicities in physiological activities, biologists initially believed (in the 1950s) that these were synonymous with health and youth and that chaotic behaviours were associated with pathological states and old age. This is far from the case: widely varying cardiac rhythms are more easily tolerated by young subjects than by ill or old people. Moreover, strictly periodic behaviours can emerge in the course of illnesses, for example with the variation in the number of leucocytes, which is highly irregular in healthy subjects and becomes periodic in certain types of leukaemia. In short, chaotic behaviours are an intrinsic characteristic of the rhythms of the living organism, in which both of these rhythms–chaos and rhythmicity–are combined. Everything that we know at present about oscillators can be used in the understanding of biological rhythms. There are interactions between rhythms and these introduce non-linearities.[35]

Before presenting the simplified model of fluctuations in psychic rhythms, I must make some important qualifications: 1. the biological universe has its own laws and it may seem scientifically meaningless to apply physical laws without any modification, particularly in relation to laws of functioning of the psychic apparatus and human subjectivity. It is for this reason that I considered that the construction of a model of this kind could relate only to the (energic) economic viewpoint. 2. Many biological dynamics contain a greater or lesser component of noise; that is, randomness. The complex problem to resolve is the dissociation that characterises the interrelations between noise and intrinsic dynamic behaviours; it is understandable that in the context of the psyche, the concept of randomness occupies an important position. These difficulties notwithstanding, I have sought to develop a preliminary model with the aid of a mathematician colleague.[36]

Presentation of the model

To begin with the explanatory variables: the starting point for the model is a (regular) exponential absorption of the initial trauma induced by a sum of excitations. These propositions accord with the models of S. Freud & P. Marty. These hypotheses can be formulated in the following equation that accounts for the initial trauma $(QE(0))$; that is, the quantity of excitations induced by the event:

$$QE'(t) + QE(t) = 0.$$

This corresponds to the development illustrated by the following graph, in which the quantities of excitation are absorbed after a certain period of time (Fig. 1).

This development is ideal and corresponds to an almost perfect work of mental elaboration by the psychic apparatus: all the excitations are absorbed. In reality, this development is "corrected or disturbed" by two phenomena:

- A process of "memorisation", which increases the quantity of excitations connected with the existing traumatic event (this

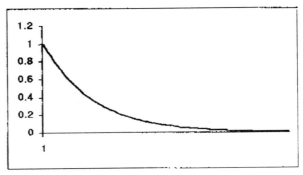

Figure 1

relates to Freud's theory of trauma); this memorisation thus positively boosts the quantity of excitations. This phenomenon is expressed by the equation $f(QE(t-t_1))$, in which t_1 represents the delay caused by memorisation. *In fact, the existing trauma reactivates the memory of conscious and unconscious past traumas.*

- An elaborative work of the psychic apparatus that diminishes the quantity of excitations, but this work influences previous excitations; this hypothesis is consistent with theory and clinical practice since it takes account of the usual processes of the work of the preconscious, which links excitations with past and existing mental representations through impulses that move back and forth between past and present. This phenomenon of psychic work is represented by the equation $g(QE(t-t_2))$ in which t_2 is less than t1: $t_2 < t_1$. A proportion of the traumatic excitations is absorbed by the psychic work.

The equation for the development of the quantities of excitations thus becomes:

$$QE'(t) + QE(t) = f(QE(t-t_1)) - g(QE(t-t_2))$$

In the second graph, the trajectory of the curves was inspired by a research study conducted by Michael Mackey and Leon Glass at the department of physiology at McGill University on "Oscillation and chaos in physiological control systems": control of the respiratory system and haematopoiesis.

The research by Mackey & Glass has the same objective as our own, namely to demonstrate that simple mathematical models that describe physiological systems can help to predict (periodic and aperiodic) dynamic instabilities that resemble those encountered in illnesses. In the curve in Figure 2, we can observe that the quantity of excitations initially increases, reinforced by an amplifying effect of the memory until a point beyond which there is a reversal: in the zone adjacent to 1, regardless of the intensity of traumatic excitations, the phenomenon reaches a saturation point.

The construction of the model is supplemented by the following equation, which introduces "b" and "c" as two inherent parameters of the psychic structure; here I am referring back to all Marty's works on mentalisation and the constitution of psychic structures. The value of b is > 1 for f and < 1 for g. For the sake of simplicity, we

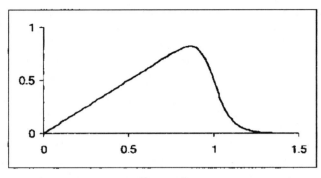

Figure 2

have arbitrarily chosen (b for g) = (b for f)/3 in the model simulations. Using this set of equations and parameters, it is possible to establish long-term developments in the quantity of excitations for different values of parameter b; as we can observe from the five following b values, we have used a value of b = 1.65 to indicate the presence of an attractor and instability in accordance with the psychosomatic hypotheses concerning the destiny of excitations. The higher the b parameter, the greater is the manifestation of instability. The existing quantity of excitations is boosted by the memorisation of excitations connected with the previous trauma, revealing in some psychic structures the incapacity to elaborate the quantities of excitations. *In Appendix 1, I have described five different structures with increasingly limited capacities for psychic elaboration.* The flooding of the psychic apparatus by large quantities of excitations creates a dynamic instability of a psychic nature, which is transmitted to the somatic realm, predominantly destabilising the hypothalamic function. This leads to a processing of excitations at the somatic level: *the body displaces the mind.*

In the set of graphs presented, the value of the initial traumatic impact is equal to 0.5 and only a single impact is taken into consideration. It can thus be understood that in the reality of human lives, traumas may be numerous and have varying intensities, which can lead to highly complex mathematical models in the quest for a better understanding of the reality of clinical and psychotherapeutic observations.

For b=1.5

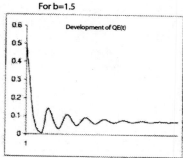 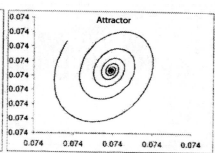

For b=1.6

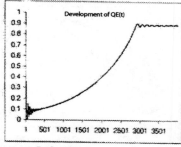 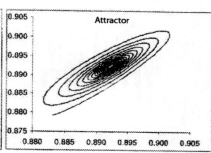

For b=1.65

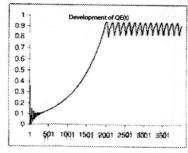 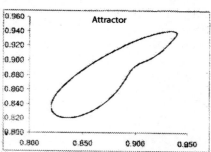

For b=1.7

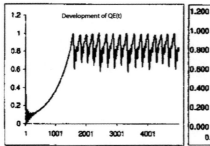
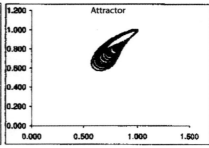

For b=1.8

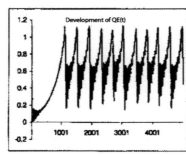
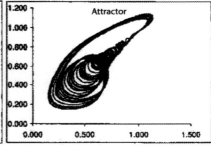

NOTES

1. Gilles Mauffrey is a mathematician who is head of the IT department and consultant at the Hautes Études Commerciales business school, with whom I formulated a mathematical model of fluctuations in psychic energy.

2. See Chapter 5 for a discussion of the ethno-psychoanalytic and psychosomatic dimension in immigrant patients.

3. These are peptic ulcers, rheumatic arthritis, hyperthyroidism, essential hypertension, bronchial asthma, neurodermatitis and thyrotoxicosis. The term "psychosomatic affection" was proposed by Halliday and, in contrast to this, Alexander emphasised that a psychological causal approach was inadequate and that "All available evidence ... points to multi-causal explanations in all branches of medicine" (1950, p. 51).

4. From 1987, with Pierre Marty I undertook the first epidemiological studies on approximately 321 patients in our hospital using the "psychosomatic classification"–see Bibliography for the references to these works that I continued alone after his death.

5. I am referring to Freud's theory of deferred action (*Nachträglichkeit*)–the modification of psychic material.

6. This is a concept defined by Helmholtz in 1862–a phenomenon in which a physical system is made to vibrate at a very different frequency from its natural frequency (or frequencies); the effect–initially weak–grows as the excitational frequency approaches a natural frequency, until it goes on to reach a very high

amplitude of vibration (amplitude of resonance) when one stands exactly at one of the natural frequencies.

7. This concept of "mental representation" does not correspond to the conception developed by Freud in his metapsychology.

8. The fields of knowledge relating to "the bio-regulatory and social domain seem to have an affinity for the systems in the ventromedial sector, while systems in the dorsolateral region appear to align themselves with domains which subsume knowledge of the external world (entities such as objects and people, their actions in space-time; language; mathematics, music)" Damasio, 1995, p. 183.

9. Object relations are the relations between a subject and an object; here, the newborn constitutes the subject. Spitz distinguishes three stages in the development of the object: a pre-objectal or objectless stage, a stage that is the precursor to the object and the stage of the libidinal object as such.

10. In *The Interpersonal World of the Infant* (1985), Daniel Stern developed a more complex model than that of Spitz based on neuronal foundations that take account of recent developments in the neurosciences. His contribution in no way undermines the concept of the coenaesthetic organisation.

11. This concept should be included in the expanded notion of *somatic compliance*.

12. This case reported by this author has been summarised and commentated by us in the context of psychoanalytic psychosomatic theory.

13. Freud was confronted with the problem of the operational conditions of the "neuronic apparatus" (first name), since if we adopt the principle of a complete energic discharge of neurones (inertia principle) what then becomes of the constancy principle that is intended to maintain an adequate provision of energy to satisfy "the urgency of life?" Freud thus makes the constancy principle a secondary function of the inertia principle, thereby connecting the inertia principle with free energy and thus with the primary process and the constancy principle with bound energy (secondary process). In *Beyond the Pleasure Principle* (1920), Freud amplifies and modifies the theoretical structure, since the constancy principle is stated to be the foundation of the pleasure principle, with an ambiguous equivalence between the inertia principle and the constancy principle. Freud thus introduces at the drive level the distinction between the death drives, tending to the absolute reduction of tensions and the life drives, tending to maintain and create units of life at a higher level of tension.

14. The "quantum" of excitations is a term often used by both psychoanalysts and psychosomaticians; taken from physics, the term "quantum" has an entirely different conceptual meaning here. Rather than quantum physics, this is a reference to a specific quantity of excitations. I have, however, kept this familiar expression to psychoanalytic readers in inverted commas.

15. Actual symptoms are mainly somatic in nature; the origin of these neuroses is to be sought in disorders of the sexual life in the present–Freud distinguishes anxiety neurosis, neurasthenia and hypochondria as actual neuroses.

16. The repetition compulsion pre-dates the pleasure-unpleasure principle; these two principles, which are both preservative in nature, seek to eliminate the consequences of the stimulations that introduce a disturbance. The repetition compulsion sets about absorbing external stimulations, whereas the pleasure-unpleasure principle eases the internal stimulations of the former.

17. I am using the concepts put forward in the previous chapter concerning the assessment of individual mentalisation and thus the wealth of imaginative experience. This is assessed in a subjective way by the practitioner in the light of his clinical experience; Marty himself does not use the terms "hypersymbolic" and "hyposymbolic".

18. "Progressive disorganisation can be defined as the destruction of the individual's libidinal organisation at a specific point in time. It partly corresponds to Freud's concept of "defusion" and the qualification "progressive" indicates that the retrograde impulse is never impeded by any viable regressive system. In most cases, the disorganisation leads to a somatisation process. Clinical phenomena are among the manifestations of the death instinct".

19. "It is in these depressions that have neither an object, nor self-accusation, nor even conscious guilt that the sense of reduced self-worth and narcissistic injury electively gravitates towards the somatic domain. Such a picture, for us, is evidently associated with precarity in the mental work".

20. "The concept of operative life is used in preference to "operative thought" to refer more specifically to the reduction in thought confronted with the importance of behaviours. The few representations that seem to exist are (like dreams) impoverished and repetitive and are characterised by current and factual material".

21. This was a stage-1 melanoma, but no monitoring regime appeared to have been established because the patient made no reference to this. As I recall, a consensus conference was held on this subject in 1996, which recommended twice-yearly monitoring for two years, then yearly for three years when the melanoma is *in situ*. When Breslow's index is higher than 1.5 mm, monitoring should take place four times a year for five years, then yearly for the rest of life.

22. Once again in this case, we can observe that somatosis and psychosis emerge at the same archaic intersection.

23. This involves the above-mentioned core of the coenaesthetic organisation of fundamental bio-regulation.

24. Cf. the explanatory model in the Appendix of the various paths leading to chaos.

25. I should like to thank Alexandre Har, a trainee psychotherapist in the department in which I had a psychosomatic consultation, for his permission to

use this patient's case, to whom he had in fact given another surname; such was the unusual destiny of this patient, who for administrative reasons had not received his parents' surname. I bear sole responsibility for the summary and the psychoanalytic and psychosomatic commentaries on the case presented, as well as the historical and anthropological analyses (cultural differences). I have given my colleague's patient a different name for confidentiality reasons.

26. Stage A is a clinical latency period in which the signs of primary infection manifest; it can last from two to ten years during which the viral replication continues. In stage B, minor symptoms appear; stage C, the AIDS stage, is defined by the emergence of opportunistic infections or a tumour belonging to a defined list including Kaposi's sarcoma and lymphomas. Infections can include: pulmonary pneumocystosis, toxoplasmosis, oesophageal candidiasis and cytomegalovirus infections.

27. As a Professor of Economic Science in addition to my skills as a psychosomatician, for many years I taught the course in "Economic fluctuations and growth" in both France and the United States.

28. The stages are as follows: shock-sideration-denial; anger; bargaining; depression; acceptance of death.

29. The concept of a native geographical country comprises aspects that are often traumatic: I was born in Algeria, in a country that was said to be a group of French departments. That is what I learnt as a child at primary school. Much later on, when Algeria gained independence, this reality had a powerful impact on me and suddenly raised the problem of the national existence of my native country. Where was it located? It is only my memories that restore some of its reality to me. My cultural origins with multiple roots enabled me to overcome these problems by transcending these national barriers. However, what is the situation for children from the second generation of emigrants?

30. My first article in 1955 on the subject of political economy refers to the *Muqaddimah*, one of the treatises of this famous scholar.

31. The Talmud is a vast collection of oral law. There are two Talmuds (the word comes from the verb *"lammed"*, to teach): The Jerusalem Talmud and the more extensive Babylon Talmud. It comprises two parts: a haggadic part (moral tales and teachings) and a legislative part or halakha.

32. The Zohar or Book of Splendour is a mystical commentary on the Torah (five books of Moses) and is the principal work of the Kabbalah.

33. Berbers of the Aurès plateau.

34. The soft sciences or human sciences, although psychoanalysis is at present unique among the human sciences in its remoteness from the quantitative methodologies used in other scientific fields.

35. The characteristic that underlies the term "non-linearity" is that of systems in which the effects are disproportionate to the magnitude of the causes.

36. Professor Gilles Mauffrey at the Hautes Études Commerciales Business School.

BIBLIOGRAPHY

Alexander, F. (1950). *Psychosomatic Medicine: Its Principles and Applications* with a chapter on the functions of the sexual apparatus and their disturbances by Therese Benedek. New York: Norton.

Ader, R., Felten, D., & Cohen, N. (Eds) (1991). *Psychoneuroimmunology* (2nd ed). New York: Academic Press.

Alpert, S. (1990). Growth, Thermogenesis and Hyperphagia. *AM J Clin Nutr*, 52: 784–92.

Amar, N., Couvreur, C. & Hanus, M. (1994). *Le Deuil*. In: Monographie de la Revue Française de Psychanalyse. Paris: P.U.F.

Amrouche Taos. (1987). *Le grain magique, contes, poèmes et proverbes berbères de Kabylie*. Paris: Ed. La Découverte.

Anzieu, D. (1975). *L'auto-analyse de Freud, et les découvertes de la psychanalyse*. Paris: P.U.F.

Anzieu, D. (1990). *L'épiderme nomade et la peau psychique*. Paris: ed. Apsygée.

Anzieu, D. (1994). *Le penser, du Moi-peau au Moi-pensant*. Paris: Dunod.

Aristote (1993). *De l'âme, traduction inédite par Richard Bodéus*. Paris: éd. Flammarion.

Atlan, H. (1986). *A tort et à raison, intercritique de la science et du mythe*. Paris: Ed. du Seuil.

Atlan, H. (1979). *Entre le cristal et la fumée, essai sur l'organisation du vivant*. Paris: Ed. du Seuil.

Balint, M. (1952). *Primary Love and Psycho-Analytic Technique*. London: Hogarth.

Basdevant, A. (1989). L'obésité. *Les Dossiers du praticien, Impact Médecin, n°39*.

Bergé, P., Pomeau, Y. & Dubois-Gance, M. (1997). *Des rythmes au chaos*. Paris: Odile Jacob.

Bergeret, J. (1984). *La violence fondamentale*. Paris: Dunod.

Bergeret, J. (1993). Psychanalyse et universalité interculturelle. *Revue Française de Psychanalyse*, Tome LVII, Juillet-Septembre: 809–839.

Bertalanffy, L. von (1968). *General Systems Theory*. New York: Braziller.

Bick, E. (1968). The experience of the skin in early object-relations. *Int. J. Psychoanal. 49*: 484–486.

Bion, W.R. (1974). *L'attention et l'interprétation*. Payot, Paris.

Botella, C. & S. (1992). Névrose traumatique et cohérence psychique. *Revue Française de Psychosomatique, n°2*: 25–36.

Botella, C. & S. (1995). Sur le processus analytique du perceptif aux causalités psychiques. *Rev. Franç. Psychanal., 2*: 349–366.

Bowlby, J. (1969). *Attachment*. Vol. 1. London: The Tavistock Institute of Human Relations.

Braconnier, A., Chiland, C., Choquet, M. & Pomarede, R. (1995). *Dépression, adolescentes, adolescents*. Paris: Ed. Bayard.

Boureau, F. (1988). *Pratique du traitement de la douleur*. Paris: Doin.

Breuer, J. & Freud, S. (1893–95). *Studies on Hysteria. S.E. 2*.

Cannon, W. B. (1935). Stresses and strains of homeostasis. *Amer. J. Med. SC., 189*: 1–1.

Cannon, W. B. (1914). The interrelations of emotions as suggested by recent physiological researches. Amer. J. Psychol., 25: 256–282.

Cannon, W. B. (1928). The mechanism of emotional disturbances of bodily functions. *N. England J. Med., 198*: 877–884.

Cassuto, J-P., Pesce, A. & Quaranta, J-F. (1996). *Le S.I.D.A., N°2332, "Que sais-je?", 6° édition*. Paris: P.U.F.

Charrier, D. (1986). *Hypertension artérielle essentielle, une réflexion sur sa prise en charge*. Paris: Ellipses.

Chemouilli, H. (1976). *Une diaspora méconnue: Les juifs d'Algérie*. Paris: I.M.P.

Chouraqui, A. (1972). *La Saga des Juifs en Afrique du Nord*. Paris: Hachette.

Claverie, L., Maillard, D. & Warnet, J. (1997). Mise au point en matière de prise en charge du malade cancéreux. *Gynécologie et Psychosomatique, n°18*: 24–29.

Clément, K., Basdevant, A., Guy-Grand, B. & Froguel, P. (1977). Génétique et obésité. *Mini-revue CNRS EP, Institut Pasteur, Sang Thrombose Vaisseaux, 9*: 487–96.

Collectif. (1993). Petit Manuel de Psychothérapie des Migrants, *Nouvelle Revue d'Ethnopsychiatrie, n°20*. Grenoble: La Pensée Sauvage.

Collectif. (1991). Objets, Charmes et Sorts. *Nouvelle Revue d'Ethnopsychiatrie, n°16*. Grenoble: La Pensée Sauvage.

Cohen, J.D. & Servan-Schreiber, D. (1992). Introduction to neural network models in psychiatry. *Psychiatry Annals 22*: 113–118.

Cooper, C.L. (1988). *Stress and Breast cancer*. London: John Wiley and Sons.

Couvreur, C., Oppenheimer, A., Perron, R. & Schaeffer, J. (1996). Psychanalyse, neurosciences, cognitivismes. *Revue Française de Psychanalyse*, monographie. Paris: P.U.F.

Damasio, A.R. (1995). *Descartes' Error: Emotion, Reason and the Human Brain*. London and Basingtoke: Picador (Macmillan).

Dennet, D. (1991). *Consciousness Explained*. Boston: Little Brown.

Descartes, R. (1996). *Les passions de l'âme*. Paris: Mille et Une nuits.

Devereux, G. (1959). *Art and Mythology, Methodology in Cross-Cultural Personality Study*. Second Geza Rohem Memorial Award Lecture.

Dolto, F. (1984). *L'image inconsciente du corps*. Paris: Seuil.

Doutre, M.S. (1990). Lupus érythémateux chronique, lupus cutané subaigu. *La Revue du Praticien, La maladie lupique, n°21*: 1930–1934.

Doutté, E. (1984). *Magie et Religion dans l'Afrique du Nord* (1ère édit. 1908). Paris: J. Maisonneuve et P. Geuthner.

Duparc, F. (1986). La peur des Sirènes, de la violence à la castration chez la femme. *Revue Française de Psychanalyse, 2*: 697–725.

Edelman, G.M. (1992). *Bright Air, Brilliant Fire: On the matter of Mind.* New York: Basic Books.

Engel, G.L. (1977). The need for a new model: a challenge for biomedicine. *Science, 196*: 129.

Fain, M. & Dejours, C. (1984). *Corps malade et corps érotique.* Paris: Masson.

Fain, M. (1992). La vie opératoire et les potentialités de névrose traumatique. *Revue Française de Psychosomatique, n°2*: 5–24.

Fawzy, F.I. & coll. (1995). Critical review of psychosocial interventions in cancer care. *Arch. Gen. Psychiatr., 52*: 100–112.

Feinleib, M., Levine, S., Scotch, N. & Kannel, W. B. (1978). The relationship of psychosocial factors to coronary heart disease in the Framingham study. Prevalence of coronary heart disease. *Amer. J. Epidemiol., 107*: 384–402.

Feinleib, M., Levine, S., Scotch, N. & Kannel, W. B. (1980). The relationship of psychosocial factors in the Framingham study. Eight years incidence of coronary heart disease. *Amer. J. Epidemiol., 111*: 37–58.

Ferenczi, S. (1929). The unwelcome child and his death instinct. In *Final Contributions* (pp. 100–102). London: Hogarth, 1955.

Flanders-Dunbar, H. (1935). *Emotions and bodily changes.* New York: Columbia University Press.

Frankel, J.B. (1998). Ferenczi's Trauma Theory. *The American Journal of Psychoanalysis, Vol. 58*: 41–62.

Fougereau, M. (1995). *L'immunologie.* Paris: P.U.F. "Que sais-je?" n°1358.

Freud, S. (1923). *The Ego and the Id. S.E.* 19.

Freud, S. (1894). *The neuro-psychoses of defence. S.E.* 3.

Freud, S. (1985). *The Complete Letters of Sigmund Freud to Wilhelm Fliess* (1897–1904). Translated and edited by Jeffrey Moussaieff Masson, Cambridge (Massachusetts) and London: The Belknap Press of Harvard University Press, 1985.

Freud, S. (1905). *Fragment of an analysis of a case of hysteria ("Dora"). S.E.* 7.

Freud, S. (1910). *The psycho-analytic view of psychogenic disturbance of vision. S.E.* 11.

Freud, S. (1912–1913). *Totem and Taboo. S.E.* 13.

Freud, S. (1917). *Mourning and melancholia. S.E.* 14.

Freud, S. (1919). *"A child is being beaten". A contribution to the study of sexual perversions. S.E.* 17.

Freud, S. (1920). *Beyond the Pleasure Principle. S.E.* 18.

Freud, S. (1926). *Inhibitions, Symptoms and Anxiety. S.E.* 20.

Freud, S. (1933). *New Introductory Lectures. S.E.* 22.

Friedman, M. & Rosenman, R.H. (1959). Association of specific overt behaviour pattern with blood and cardiovascular findings. *J. Amer. Med. Assn., 169*: 1085–1096.

Friedman, M. & Ulmer, D. (1984). *Treating type A behaviour and your heart.* New York: Ballantine books.

Ghanta, V., Hiramoto, R., Solvason, H. & Spector, N. (1985). Neural and environmental influences on neoplasia and conditioning of NK activity. *Journal of Immunology, 135 (2)*: 848s–852s.

Gachelin, G. (1995). Psychosomatique et modèles en immunologie. *Revue Française de psychosomatique, n°8*: 7–23.

Galatzer-Levy, R.M. (1988). On working through a model from artificial intelligence. *J. Amer. Psychoanal. Assn, 36*: 125–151.

Galien. (1994). *Œuvres médicales choisies, de l'utilité des parties du corps humain, et des faculté naturelles, des lieux affectés, de la méthode thérapeutique, à Glaucun (T.I & II).* Paris: Gallimard.

Gille, E. (1994). *Le crabe sur la banquette arrière.* Paris: *coll. Folio,* Mercure de France.

Glaser, R. & Kiecolt-Glaser, J. (1991). Modulation of the cellular immune response. *Clinical Immunology Newsletter, 11*: 101–105.

Gleick, J. (1988). *Chaos: Making a New Science.* London: Heinemann.

Globus, G. (1992). Toward a noncomputational cognitive neuroscience. *J. Cog. Neurosci. 4*: 299–310.

Globus, G., Arpaia, J.P. (1994). Psychiatry and the new dynamics. *Biol. Psychiatry 35*: 352–364.

Glover, E. (1956). *The Birth of the Ego.* New York: George Allen & Unwin Ltd.

Graham, J.D.P. (1945). High blood pressure after battle, *Lancet, 1*: 239–240.

Green, A. (1993). *Le travail du négatif.* Paris: Les éditions de minuit.

Green, A. (1996). Cognitivisme, neurosciences, psychanalyse, un dialogue difficile. In: *Débats de psychanalyse. Revue Fr. Psychan*: 61–70.

Guibert, H. (1990). *A l'ami qui ne m'a pas sauvé la vie.* Paris: Gallimard, Folio.

Guibert, H. (1992). *Cytomégalovirus, journal d'hospitalisation.* Paris: éd. du Seuil.

Guillemin, R., Vargo, T., Rossier, J., Minick, S., Ling, N., Vale, W. & Bloom, F. (1977). Beta endorphin and adrenocorticotropin are secreted concomitantly by the pituitary gland. *Science*, 197: 1368–1369.

Guillerault, G. (1996). *Les Deux Corps du Moi, schéma corporel et image du corps en psychanalyse.* Paris: Gallimard.

Guir, J. (1983). *Psychosomatique et cancer.* Paris: Point hors ligne.

Hall, N., McGillis, J., Spangelo, B. & Goldstein, A. (1985). Evidence that thymosins and other biologic response modifiers can function as neuroactive immunotransmitters. *The Journal of Immunology, 135 (2)*: 806s–811s.

Hardy, P. (1993). *Epidémiologie des associations entre troubles mentaux et affections organiques.* Paris: P.U.F.

Haynal, A. & Pasini, W. (1978). *Médecine psychosomatique (2nd, 1984).* Paris: Masson.

Hippocrate de Cos. (1994). *De l'art médical,* traduction d'Emile Littré. Paris: Le livre de Poche Librairie Générale Française.

Hofstede, G. (1982/1983). National Cultures in Four Dimensions: a research-based theory of cultural differences among nations. *International Studies of management and organization, Vol. XII, n°1–2 (Winter)*: 46–74.

Holmes, T. & Rahe, T. (1967). The social readjustment rating scale. *Journal of Psychosomatic Research, 11*: 213–18.

James, W. (1998). *The Principles of Psychology.* (2 Vols.) Thoemmes Press UK & Maruzen Co. Ltd. Tokyo (1890).

Jasmin, C.l., Lé, M.G., Marty, P. & Herzberg, R. (1990). Evidence for a link between certain psychological factors and the risk of breast cancer in a case-control study. *Annals of Oncology, I*: 22–29.

Jeammet, Ph., Reynaud, M. & Consoli, S.M. (1996). *Psychologie médicale.* Paris: Masson.

JIM (1996). *Journal International de Médecine.* No. 367, p. ix.

Jones, E. (1953). *Sigmund Freud: Life and Work. The Formative Years and the Great Discoveries, 1856–1900.* Vol. 1. New York: Basic Books.

Jones, E. (1957). *Sigmund Freud: Life and Work. The Last Phase 1919–1939.* Vol. 3. London: Hogarth Press.

Kabat-Zin, J. (1990). *Full Catastrophe Living: Using the Wisdom of Your Body and Mind to Face Stress, Pain and Illness.* New York: Bantam Doubleday Dell Publishing Group, Inc. (Dell Publishing).

Klein, M., Heimann, P., Isaacs, S. & Rivière, J. (1952). *Developments in Psycho-Analysis.* London: The Hogarth Press Ltd and The Institute of Psycho-Analysis.

Kohut, H. (1971). *The Analysis of the Self.* New York: International Universities Press, Inc.

Kohn, A. (1990). *Pour le pire et ... pour le meilleur, un cas de lupus érythémateux.* Paris: publication personnelle de l'auteur.

Kreisler, L. (1987). *Le nouvel enfant du désordre psychosomatique.* Toulouse: Privat.

Kübler-Ross, E. (1995). *Death is of Vital Importance.* New York: Station Hill Press, Barrytown.

Lacoste-Dujardin, C. (1970). *Le conte Kabyle, étude ethnologique.* Paris: François Maspero.

Lapin, B.A. & Cherkovich, G.M. (1971). Environmental Change causing the Development of Neuroses and Corticovisceral Pathology in Monkeys. In: Levi (ed.), *Society, Stress and Disease* (pp. 226–280). London: Oxford University Press.

Laplanche, J. & Pontalis, J-B. (1973). *The Language of Psycho-Analysis.* Translated by Donald Nicholson-Smith. London: Hogarth Press. (1971). *Vocabulaire de la psychanalyse.* Paris: P.U.F.

LeShan, L.L. (1959). Psychological states as factors in the development of malignant disease: a critical review. *Journal of the National Cancer Institute, 22:* 1–18.

Loo, R. & Loo, H. (1986). *Le stress permanent.* Paris: Masson.

Lorenz, E. (1963). Deterministic nonperiodic flow. *Journal of the Atmospheric Sciences, n°20:* 130–141.

Mackey, M. & Glass, L. (1977). Oscillation and chaos in physiological control systems. *Science,* Vol. 197: 287–89.

Mahler, M. (1952). On child psychosis and schizophrenia—autistic and symbiotic infantile psychoses, *Psychoanalytic Study of the Child,* 7: 286–305.

Maïmonide. (1135–1204). Le traité de l'asthme, traduit pour la première fois d'après le texte hébraïque par le Prof. Susmann

Munthner et le Dr Isidore Simon (1963). *Revue d'histoire de la médecine hébraïque, n°62*: 171–188; (1964). *n°63*: 5–14; (1965). *n°67*: 5–15.

Mason, I.W. (1968). A review of psychoendocrine research on the pituary-adrenal cortical system. *Psychosom. Med.*, 30: 576–607.

McDougall, J. (1991). *Theatres of the Mind*. London: Routledge.

McDougall, J. (1989). *Theaters of the Body. A Psychoanalytic Approach to Psychosomatic Illness*. New York: Norton.

McDougall, J. (1996). *The Many Faces of Eros*. London: Free Association Books.

Marty, P. (1980). *L'ordre psychosomatique, T. 2*. Paris: Payot.

Marty, P. & Stora, J. B. (1989). *Psychosomatiques*, Beyrouth: ed. Beyrouth, (en langue arabe).

Marty, P. & Stora, J.B. (1988). La Classification psychosomatique Marty/ Ipso, méthode d'aide au diagnostic des organisations psychosomatiques et des maladies somatiques. Lausanne: *Médecine et Hygiène*.

Marty, P. & Stora, J.B. (1989). La clasificacion psicosomatica MARTY/IPSO: metodo diagnostico de las organizaciones psicosomaticas y enfermedades somaticas. *Psicoterapia Analitica, Vol. 1, n°1*: 19–31.

Marty, P. (1990). *La psychosomatique de l'adulte*. Paris: P.U.F. (Que sais-je? n° 1850).

Marty, P., De M'Uzan, M. & David, C. (1994). *L'investigation psychosomatique, sept observations cliniques*. Paris: P.U.F.

Marty, P., Fain, M., De M'Uzan, M., David, C. (1968). Le cas Dora et le point de vue psychosomatique. *Revue française de Psychanalyse, Vol. 32*: 679–714.

Mitrani, J.L. (1995). Toward an understanding of unmentalized experience, *The Psychoanalytic Quaterly, Volume LXIV, n°1*: 68–112.

Montel, M. (1994). *Un mal imaginaire*. Paris: Les éditions de Minuit.

Moulinier, A. (1996). Atteinte du système nerveux central. In: S. Hefez (Ed.), *Sida et vie psychique*. Paris: La Découverte.

Nathan, T. (1986). *La folie des autres, traité d'ethnopsychiatrie clinique*. Paris: Ed. Dunod.

Nathan, T. (1988). *Psychanalyse païenne, essais ethnopsychanalytiques*. Paris: ed. Dunod.

Nathan, T. (1994). *L'influence qui guérit*. Paris: Odile Jacob.

Noble, N., A. (1989). Psychosocial and behavioural factors in myocardial infraction and sudden cardiac death. In: S. Cheren, *Psychosomatic Medicine* (pp. 611–659). Madison (CT): International Un. Press.

Nunn, T. H. (1822). *Cancer of the breast*. London: J. & A. Churchill.

Olds, D.D. (1994). Connectionism and Psychoanalysis. *J. Amer. Psychoanal. Assn., 42*: 581–611.

Pédinielli, J-L. (1992). *Psychosomatique et alexithymie*. Paris: P.U.F. coll. Nodules.

Pendergrass, E. (1961). Host Resistance and Other Intangibles in the Treatment of Cancer. *American Journal of Roengenology, 85*: 891–896.

Piesse, L. (1888*). Algérie et Tunisie*. Coll. Guides-Joanne. Paris: Hachette.

Pillonel, J. (1996). Epidémiologie du sida et l'infection à VIH. In: S. Hefez (Ed.), *Sida et vie psychique*. Paris: La Découverte.

Prigogine, I. & Stengers. (1984). *Order out of Chaos*. London: Heinemann.

Ravussin, E. & Swinburn, B.A. (1992). Physiopathologie de l'obésité. *The Lancet, éd. française, novembre*: 25–34.

Reinberg, A. (1989). *Les rythmes biologiques*. Paris: P.U.F.

Riviere, J. (Ed.) (1952). *Developments in Psycho-Analysis*. London: Hogarth Press.

Rivolier, J. (1989). *L'homme stressé*. Paris: Presses Universitaires de France.

Rodado, J. & Rendon M. (1996). Can Artificial Intelligence Be of Help to Psychoanalysis. *The American journal of Psychoanalysis, Vol. 56, No. 4*: 395–413.

Rosenberg, B. (1991). *Masochisme mortifère et masochisme gardien de la vie*. Monographie de la Revue française de Psychanalyse. Paris: P.U.F.

Rosenberg, B. (1995). Relire Marty. De la dépression essentielle à la somatisation: réflexions sur le rôle du masochisme dans ce mouvement. *Revue Française de Psychosomatique, n°8*: 91–105.

Rosenman, R.H. (1978). Role of Type A behavior pattern in the pathogenesis of ischemic heart disease and modification for prevention. *Adv. Cardiol., 25*: 35–46.

Rosner, F. (1984). *La médecine de Maïmonide*. In: Mishne Torah, traduction de Daniel et Ariel Beresniak. New York: Britt International Publications.

Rossi, E.L. (1993). *The Psychobiology of Mind-Body Healing: New Concepts of Therapeutic Hypnosis*. New York: WW. Norton & Company, Inc.

Rouach, D. (1990). *"IMMA"*, *Rites, coutumes et croyances chez la femme juive en Afrique du Nord*. Paris: Maisonneuve & Larose.

Ruelle, D. (1991). *Chance and Chaos*. Princeton, NJ and Oxford: Princeton University Press.

Ruelle, D. & Takens, F. (1971). On the Nature of Turbulence. *Commun. Math. Phys.* 20: 167–192: 23: 343–344 (1971).

Sami-Ali (1987). *Penser le somatique, imaginaire et pathologie*. Paris: Bordas.

Schilder, P. (1968). *L'image du corps, Etude des forces constructives de la psyche*. Paris: Gallimard.

Schmale, A.H. & Iker, H. (1966). The psychological setting of uterine cervical cancer. *Annals of New York Acad. Sci.* 125: 807.

Schur, M. (1975). *La mort dans la vie de Freud*. Paris: Gallimard.

Selye, H. (1974). *Stress without distress*. New York: Signet.

Selye, H. (1976). *The stress of life*. New York: McGraw Hill.

Sifnéos, P.E. (1993). The prevalence of alexithymic characteristics in psychosomatic patients. *Psychother. Psychosom.*, 22: 255–262.

Simonton, O.C. & Matthews-Simonton, S. (1978). *Getting well again, a step-by-step, self-help guide to overcoming cancer for patients and their families*. Los Angeles: J.P. Tarcher, Inc.

Sokal, A. & Bricmont, J. (1997). *Impostures intellectuelles*. Paris: Odile Jacob.

Solomon, G. (1985). The emerging field of psychoneuroimmunology with a special note on AIDS, *Advances*, 2 (Winter: 6–19).

Spinoza, B. (1996). *The Ethics*. Edited and translated by Edwin Curley. With an Introduction by Stuart Hampshire. London: Penguin.

Spitz, R. (1965). *The First Year of Life: A Psychoanalytic Study of Normal and Deviant Development of Object Relations*. New York: International Universities Press.

Stanley Cheren, M.D. (1989). *Psychosomatic Medicine, Theory, Physiology and Practice*, Vol. 1 & 2. Madison (CT): International University Press, Inc.

Stein, M., Keller, S. & Schleifer; S. (1985). Stress and immunomodulation: The role of depression and neuroendocrine function. *The Journal of Immunology, 135(2)*: 827s–833s.

Stern, D.N. (1985). *The Interpersonal World of the Infant*. London: Karnac.

Stora, J.B. (1991). *Le stress*. Paris: Presses Universitaires de France, collection "Que sais-je?" n°2575. 6° édition 2005 (Editions étrangères en espagnol, turc, portugais, arabe, grec, italien).

Stora, J.B. (1994). Sémiologie Psychosomatique. *Annales de Psychiatrie, Vol. 9, n°2*: 117–124.

Stora, J.B. (1995). Organisations mentales et maladies somatiques. *Annales de Psychiatrie, 10, n°1*: 5–11.

Stora, J.B. (1996). Indications de psychothérapie psychanalytique selon la psychopathologie: troubles psychosomatiques de l'adulte. In: A. Braconnier et D. Widlöcher (Eds.), *Psychanalyse et psychothérapies* (pp. 230–244). Paris: Flammarion.

Thomé-Renault, A. (1995). *Le traumatisme de la mort annoncée, psychosomatique et sida*. Paris: Dunod.

Tubiana, M. (1994). *Le Cancer*. Paris: P.U.F.

Tustin, F. (1990). *The Protective Shell in Children and Adults*. London: Karnac.

Van Kerkhove, C. (1990). Lupus erythematosus in childhood: effect of maternal factors beyond neonatal disease. *Clinical Rheumatology, 9, n°2*: 168–170.

Varela, F. J. (1991). *The Embodied Mind*. Boston: M.I.T Press .

Villemain, F. (1989). *Stress et immunologie*. Paris: P.U.F. Nodules.

Widlöcher, D. (1990). Neurobiologie et psychanalyse. Les opérateurs de commutation. *Revue Internationales de Psychopathologie, 2*: 235–256.

Winnicott, D.W. (1969). *L'enfant et sa famille*. Paris: Payot, 1980.

Winnicott, D.W. (1989). *Psycho-Analytic Explorations*. London: Karnac.

Winiszewski, P. & Pinget, M. (1991). Obésité, épidémiologie, étiologie, diagnostic, évolution, et pronostic, traitement. *Rev. Prat. (Paris), 41, 7*: 651–655.

Zorn, F. (1982). *Mars*. Translated by Robert and Rita Kimber. London: Pan Books.

INDEX